for *The Torturer's Wife*

"Thomas Glave, who has been compared to fellow O. Henry Award winner Richard Wright, returns with his second collection of short fiction, *The Torturer's Wife*. In passionate, disquieting prose, Glave bears eloquent witness to human traumas both large and small."
—*Bookforum*

"Interruptions, run-on sentences, and unorthodox punctuation waltz with graphic, grisly descriptions and sudden bouts of poetry. Teeming with unnamed characters and secrets galore, Glave's collection impressively and collectively presents itself as a trembling sheath barely concealing the horror and dubious complexities of modern-day life as we know it . . . there's enough human trauma and socially weighty material here to keep the serious fiction-reader wide-eyed and at full attention." —*Bay Area Reporter*

"Glave's daringly experimental but eloquent prose style, often elliptical and interspersed with lines of poetry, is a challenge. But a deep, attentive reading will yield exciting literary rewards."
—*Seattle Gay News*

"Glave's second collection is a disquieting, graphic, semiexperimental compendium examining violence and ignorance in and out of wartime . . . Glave's style, full of interruptions, ellipses, unconventional text treatments, and poemlike breaks, sends each story whirling thickly toward its end." —*Publishers Weekly*

CRITICAL PRAISE FOR THOMAS GLAVE

for *Whose Song? and Other Stories*

"These stories are never about anything but the most serious matters of existence—the mysteries of violence and desire; the 'plain old hurting sorrow' of why human beings have such trouble loving one another ... Glave is a gifted stylist ... blessed with ambition, his own voice, and an impressive willingness to dissect how individuals actually think and behave."
—New York Times Book Review

"Glave's literary temperament has been described as 'Faulknerian,' and the comparison speaks volumes. Like Faulkner, Glave can make heavy demands on a reader . . . He achieves astonishing tonal effects ... [and] has a poet's way with words."
—Washington Post

"Thomas Glave likes to plunge us right into the middle of his stories—a crowd, a conversation, a consciousness—and smack in the center of a milieu—American or Caribbean, urban or rural, usually black, often queer. The prose in this first collection is dense, dreamy ... as rich as a novel and a book of poems combined."
—Out Magazine

"This book is a gem."
—Lambda Book Report

"Glave, like so many before him at City Lights, probes the soft underbelly of love's body, ennobles it, and gives it light, all the more to make us weep when it is violently slit open ... The rape in the title story, and all the other transgressions, propose that the sensual song of humanity belongs to those who sing it and condemns as evil those who would silence it. Thomas Glave sings most eloquently, poignantly, and heroically, and those who should hear his song are everywhere."
—Bloomsbury Review

AMONG

the

BLOODPEOPLE

POLITICS AND FLESH

BY THOMAS GLAVE

Published by Akashic Books
©2013 by Thomas Glave

ISBN-13: 978-1-61775-170-7
Library of Congress Control Number: 2012954510

First printing

Front cover image: *Jesus. Es geht um die Wurst,* sculpture by
Jimmie Durham. Photograph of sculpture by Jochen Verghote.
Image reproduced with the permission of Jimmie Durham and
Het Museum van Hedendaagse Kunst Antwerpen (M HKA).

Akashic Books
PO Box 1456
New York, NY 10009
info@akashicbooks.com
www.akashicbooks.com

ALSO BY THOMAS GLAVE

―――

Whose Song? and Other Stories

Words to Our Now: Imagination and Dissent

The Torturer's Wife

*Our Caribbean: A Gathering of Lesbian and Gay Writing
from the Antilles* (Editor)

This book is dedicated with much *more* than thanks
to Norman Riley,
the greatest brother yet,
and the brothermost
friend

TABLE OF CONTENTS

———

Introduction

The Blood Work of Language
by Yusef Komunyakaa

═══

There are few voices as urgent as Thomas Glave's. In *Among the Bloodpeople,* he neither hesitates nor attempts to prepare us for the unsayable *"that"* which divorces some men and women from their Jamaican families. No sooner than a quick leap, we are wound in the bloody, necessary realities of *Politics and Flesh.* We learn the cold, hard, naked facts up front, and Glave's profound dialectical relationship to these subjects. He writes:

> Speak with them [the locals] about the more than 1,500 people murdered in Jamaica in a recent year, one of these years in the early millennium—many of the victims eviscerated by machetes and otherwise butchered—but have the courtesy and common sense not to mention that at least one of those people so brutally killed was both a beloved friend of yours and a political comrade in the fierce struggle *those* people (your people) constantly have to wage for their survival on the island.

A graphic horror opens under the sky of a place once defined as a paradise, and through the passion of language and acute imagery we feel anger and rage. But Glave's voice resonates in the plucked string holding each sentence together, an echo of James Baldwin and Jean Genet; his language carries the full freight of witness. Where Baldwin writes of being "condemned" to speak, Glave seems to race forward to accept the mantle of all the lusty details of human love and existence—arms spread wide—nimble as some guardian angel of reprobation. He writes out of need, every trembling detail unmasked. Little escapes the hawk's eye driven by a prophetic heart in the deep mix of essential renderings. Glave is a seer in the old-fashioned sense and dimension: each essay here is a body-and-soul affair. His language is seductive and regenerative, critical and humanizing, almost mathematically gauged and encompassing, and it never fails to hold us accountable. But alongside the terror we witness, moments of sheer beauty seethe out of the landscape—not as a balm, but as needful epistles of reflection.

Among the Bloodpeople is woven with a similar muscular spirit as the poetry of that other famous Jamaican, Claude McKay, in a protest sonnet such as "If We Must Die":

If we must die, let it not be like hogs
Hunted and penned in an inglorious spot,
While round us bark the mad and hungry dogs,
Making their mock at our accursed lot.

Yes, these essays pulsate with the same charged lyrical, moral authority. No one easily wriggles off the hook. But here's one agonizing difference: McKay's poem is carefully aimed at the bigotry in the USA during the fiery 1920s; Glave's *Among the Bloodpeople* is calibrated toward the provocateurs of violence against Jamaican gays and lesbians. And in this anthem of *we*, Glave portrays this confrontation with the history one carries within:

For this moment, as he ponders that beckoning water into which scores of his enslaved ancestors leapt off ships to their deaths three hundred years before, he *un*remembers the fact that this country, for the most part, has never loved him . . .

In this sense, Glave's voice is a show of force for the twenty-first century—sparked by a moral imperative. This writer calls out by name those citizens with governmental and juridical obligation who hide behind cloaks of cultivated silence, evasion, and sanction. Each is hitched to a rhetorical whipping post and shown the power of the word. At times it seems the girth and grit of language come close to curses hurled at those whose immoral violence has harmed these brothers and sisters. In so many ways, this is deep family business made of pain.

These essays are artistic and pragmatic, and Glave uses superb style as a device to ensnare those who would brutalize the people he loves and trusts in a world of scales rigged beyond any due process. He crosses borders of corporeality, timely and artfully, moving through pain-ful territories of personal history that go back genera-tions to his great-great-grandfather, and then he offers an elegiac embrace of the intangible "sound of all of them in the wind-language." Through this lyrical pursuit of truth that humanizes and subverts, the essay is Glave's weapon of choice.

The fleshed-out revelations here engage these con-temporary realities: the inability for some Jamaicans to acknowledge a gay son, or daughter, or sibling; an open letter to the prime minister; a graphic insinuation of for-bidden homosexuality; tributes to five literary forerun-ners; a poetry of deep reckoning with love; language as overlays to maps of facelessness; repression in the ivory towers of Cambridge University; picturesque moments in London as metaphor; poetic memory as the basis of empirical meaning.

The tension of poetry lives in Glave's language. And this conceit is especially highlighted in "Against Pre-ciousness" through tone and form. He questions with honed exactitude:

> People who, across the centuries, were forced to admit into their bodies the engorged parts of those who owned them for centuries. There, one's own infinite and deeply personal catalog of memory against the ultimately offensive, dishon-est, precious stink and artifice of preciousness.

The experimental moments seem naturally holistic.

Glave has done a heroic deed. Now that the cultivated climate of mayhem and violence has been clearly articulated, one sees this body of work as the blueprint for change in Jamaica. Now that the situation has been laid bare, with bones of the past edging through, there should be only one undeniable action: laws must be constituted on behalf of gays and lesbians in the Caribbean. This blueprint—this layered treatise—begs action. Clearly, something must be done in a place where violence seems so regimented and codified that it has become belief. Something has to rout the terror.

Some know of the play *The Laramie Project* based on Matthew Shepard—a twenty-one-year-old gay college student who died in 1998 on a fence in a small Wyoming town—but few people know much about what happens to these men and women in the Caribbean. Once, we could feign ignorance, but not after Glave's sharply rendered *Among the Bloodpeople*. He has gone wherever wrongheadedness goes, always focused on what seems to be the underbelly of violence in worldly localities. His is a poetry of knowledge, of body and mind, which acknowledges and confronts tribulation, a longing for gestures woven through language, baring intimate details and vows of the night nudged into the broad daylight of knowing compassion. The problem of violence seems to be located in a false, symbolic manhood still situated in a concept of colonization of the heart that should prod us to the mirror.

With US President Obama's fierce compassion for equality in his inauguration speech of January 2013, we know significant changes are in the forefront of the global psyche. Of course, especially after taking in Glave's raw and eloquent language, one hopes that there are sobering turns in the compendium of hearts and minds gathered on the edge of the Caribbean Sea. And we know there's no clemency now for passivity. There's no slipknot for escaping responsibility as witnesses. We know who the enemies of truth are, and in our silence they look like us in life and dream. But deep within each of us resides an unrelenting sense of freedom, and it is from this place that we must move forward.

Yusef Komunyakaa is the author of seventeen collections of poetry and a winner of the Pulitzer Prize. His latest collection is Testimony, A Tribute to Charlie Parker *(Wesleyan University Press). He teaches in the Graduate Creative Writing Program at New York University.*

THE CARIBBEAN
AND JAMAICA

This Jamaican Family:
The Word, and Dreams

Whether or not you accept it, you finally under-stand that this is the message, delivered by them in shouting silences and stiffened backs whenever you summon the bravery to refer, even obliquely, to *that*: the simple message that *that*, as far as they're concerned, doesn't exist in this family; that, as true, proud Jamaicans still unmoved by North American and European "for-eign" values, they will never reflect on the profundities of who you are in relation to *that*; and that by now, you should already have developed the good sense—good taste—to speak with them about other things, about anything other than *that*. Speak with them about the more than 1,500 people murdered in Jamaica in a recent year, one of these years in the early millennium—many of the victims eviscerated by machetes and otherwise butchered—but have the courtesy and common sense not to mention that at least one of those people so bru-tally killed was both a beloved friend of yours and a po-litical comrade in the fierce struggle *those* people (your people) constantly have to wage for their survival on the island. Speak with them about what the government can or cannot (or will not) do about the extreme crime rate, in Kingston especially, and share their disgust and horror over all of it, but do not—absolutely not—allude in any way to the various men-loving men whose throats were ripped open last year, or whose assorted parts were found splattered around the places in which, most commonly, they had lived: their bodies dismembered, the insider gossip went, by men who had known and desired them; men anyone in the know might have known and perhaps even "tussled with" between there and here. Men whose moistened mouths and other parts, before the dismembering, had more than likely traveled over that other man's body, inhaled its most intimate scents, and swallowed—the very beginning of the long, slow, so secret journey desired by so many. The journey into the realm of things like *but feel me now* and *all right, and take me in now, and*—all the rest of it, as always. And more, so much more.

Speak with the family about the US's presence in the Middle East: a safer subject. For you understood long ago that it would always be easier for them to deplore other people's viciousness—the US's, or Britain's—before examining and correcting their own. Listen once again to them praise, nearly without end, the church of their choice; hear them ignore your mentions of more "inclusive," homo-friendly churches operating now even in Jamaica (though mainly in Kingston); attend carefully the words of the cousin who reminds the family every chance he gets about the importance of GOD in his life, as steadfastly as he always capitalizes "GOD"; do your best not to despise utterly the cousin who, even though you showed her love and concern during her traumatizing fight with cancer and after her husband's heart attack, now routinely avoids any contact with you because she has finally divined that you are *that way*. Despite the fact that this latter cousin suspects that you might, as the Victorians would have said, somehow "interfere with" her teenaged son, cherish in your deepest heart your elderly country aunt: that highly successful seamstress trained in her craft by your mother and grandmother, who recently heard you speaking on Jamaican radio about homo matters and afterward chatted with you easily enough on the phone. Chatted, and even referred to the radio interview's content, never once failing to use, in her cracked voice, those same words she had used with you ever since your earliest days on earth: words like *darling*, like *sweetheart*. Maintain faith in that love—in the surprises of generosity and the habit, among some people, of loving broadly, bravely, all-inclusively. It will be a supreme gift, that love, to someone like you perpetually in search of Home, in search of Heart, in search of Here: *the place where I can love and, for once, be loved entirely, completely, in return. For I must run away from them all from time to time*, you have thought before and will think again, *because it hurts too much to be around their refusal to engage, I mean really engage, with who and what I am and always have been. It hurts, for if they will not/cannot love me, or can/will love me only on the condition that I somehow become not myself—choke to death part of myself, erase a part, banish to silence and nonbeing that part which they despise—well, but what to do?* (You have thought these things often enough, and felt them. Felt the fear. The anger, and the—say it!—

the loneliness. All of it so deeply painful. Yes, you know it.) *Yet here—the place that I know exists somewhere—is where I belong. I will glimpse it clearly sometimes in dreams, and know that it exists for me precisely by the feel of its warm, insistent press against me. I will know that it is here.*

Recall, do not ever forget any of it—and throughout every recollection, especially in the harshest moments still to come, remember the word.

The word, words, as in these words right here, on this page, and others. The words that can describe things like the rage you often feel (but don't necessarily express) when treated in those excommunicating, erasing ways by them; the rage that follows the always-hurt, and that knows, too well, its deepest source. The words that can provide shape to those things like *anger*; like *sorrow*; like *grief*; like *Jamaica, Jesus Christ, my people*—but also, in the best of moments, like *joy*. Joy well beyond their grasp and theft, in the words that recall (in private, in the region of the most protected dreams) the scent and taste of co-conut milk on his neck, the lick of white rum trickling along the smooth hairs below his (and where else?), and the arch of his back and glint in his eye when even now, just afterward or before, he moves that way—yes, like *that*—continuing all the while to gaze at you as you maneuver, as he prepares, until: these words that, in sorrow, in anger, in grief, in joy, will recollect and conjure, once more, him, and the possibilities associated with him.

And them? Those whom you call the bloodpeople: the people of shared DNA, shared genes and facial like-nesses, and memories of childhoods spent beneath banana trees, mango trees, soursop leaves ... The people of shared surnames that confirm the blood shared between you long after slavery and emancipation, manifested outwardly, that blood, cousin to cousin to grandparent to aunt, in a variety of skin tones. The people whom you can never truly escape—not quite in Jamaica, nor anywhere else—and whom, in spite of everything, you honestly do not yet really want—not quite—to escape. The people who, in true Jamaican middle-class style, with a few exceptions (such as your country elderly aunt, and one or two more), refuse to discuss with you *the subject*. The people who refuse to acknowledge that even in Jamaica, in fact more than ever before in Jamaica, *the subject* looms larger and ever less hidden all about them. Looms in the faces of those whom you recognize and single out as that other family (and thank God for it): the men and women who dance closely, intimately, boldly, at all those private parties held at this house or that one; who kiss, flirt, and entwine their bodies, and even sometimes live together—in Kingston, mostly, although, so far as you know, principally in the more upscale parts of town. The other/Other family that each day, even in Jamaica, steadily appears to become more tired of hiding and feeling compelled to hide, of being "other": that family. The one without which, in the face of so much anger and censoring, days and nights in Jamaica in this time would be truly intolerable, impossible, and far more threatening to the living, breathing body than they already are. Lately, with the gift of a few good friendships in that family, and with some courage, it becomes more pos-

sible to live in Jamaica with the taste of him, or someone else, in your mouth and memory, although—make
no mistake—you and all the others will have to continue living carefully. It becomes more possible, with that
other increasingly large and visible family, to live without caring so much what the ones-who-would-deny-
and-ostracize think, although, in actual (painful) love or
through some persisting sense of duty—fealty—you still
might send the bloodpeople a Christmas card; might still
drop by, though less frequently, for a bite of curry goat,
a plate of steamed fish and bammy, a drink and innocu-
ous catch-up on Boxing Day (without, while in their
home, making any references to *that*). In this present that
rapidly lopes toward another sort of future—a wider,
more daring one—family and the bloodpeople become
something else: another way of being, seeing, and—so
you hope—much less hurt. *Send that hurt across the sea,*
murmurs that old bracing voice just beneath your heart,
*in an airmail package addressed to Absolutely No One at the
farthest end of the spinning globe.* In the family of men who
press against each other and women who hold and kiss
each other, the *You are sick* excommunications will be
banished—hopefully for all time.

Soon, on another day or evening, impelled by the
faces and secrets gradually disclosed during sojourns
with the word, you will imagine as follows the shifting
portrait that will soon become memory: A portrait of
two people driving alongside the sea. Driving beneath
nodding palms. Driving in fact along one of your favorite routes in Jamaica: the slinking road out of Kingston

to Port Royal, also known as the airport road—the one over which cars race to meet descending Air Jamaica jets. The same road that pushes its sandy backside against the broad, blue-bellied sea on one side and Kingston Harbour's salty insinuations on the other. The road now stretching beneath two people driving alongside the sea and aware of each other's mouths, the slide of shoulders beneath soft cotton, and the reliable thrust of desire grasped between trembling hands. Two people driving and dreaming that something quite like joy, and more, just might be possible—knowing this time exactly how it will appear when it descends.

Now, they are savoring as they drive the dribble-juice of star apples over their lips, down the chin and over their fingers—but then all at once they are closer, moving deeper into *scents inhaled,* into *his face pressed again into my* (but that will always be a secret)—into *recollection of everything both tasted and received that once again will soon move over this other face, that, not only in dreams, so quickly becomes mine—our faces both different and the same, and the journeys between them forever and always secret. For now, here (and yes, look at it, fold what you can of yourself around it) is kinship of still another kind.*

Two people driving alongside the sea, but then who here, now, all at once bring the vehicle to a halt; then step out of the car, to walk upon the beach. Walking unseen even by the lean-limbed fishermen in their low boats way out there: unseen as one of them risks doing something, followed by laughter, to the other; as one of them risks making the other, in open daylight, feel *that;* after

which the one who did *that* presses his hand, with eyes
closed, to his face, in order to remember, without fail,
that scent. But then wait, they both think: regarding now
how the sea sucks away the sand beneath their feet in the
retreating tide. How the foam rushes in to swirl and lick,
just like that, about their ankles. The foam, now licking
higher about the exposed flesh beneath that blistering
sun so high above, as the fishermen—as they rock in
their small boats on the sea, as the foam—as a hand dares
in open daylight, impossibly, completely possibly (this
being a kind of freedom—in fact joy), to rest its palm
on that waist—resting the palm and pressing—wrapping
around to feel—

The lean-limbed fishermen, *out there*

And the sea. Swirling. Now rushing in. Foaming—

An Open Letter to the Prime Minister of Jamaica (June 2008)[1]

To the Rt. Honourable Bruce Golding,
Prime Minister of Jamaica

Dear Prime Minister Golding:

I trust that this letter will find you well. On Friday, May 23, 2008, as the opening reader at the Calabash Literary Festival in Treasure Beach, St. Elizabeth, I publicly criticized the antigay remarks you had made only a few days earlier, on May 20, on the BBC-TV show *HARDtalk*, to reporter Stephen Sackur. (You will recall having said to Mr. Sackur on the air, quite heatedly, that homosexuals will not have any place in your cabinet.[2]) I decided to critique your remarks as a citizen of Jamaica—a country that, despite its overwhelming social problems, I deeply love and believe still to be something of a democracy: that is, a nation in which, in accordance with the ideals and attainable reality of human freedom, citizens and others may voice their dissent against what they view as injustice and the missteps, and sometimes egregious errors, of governing officials; dissent that can be openly expressed without (for the most part) fear of reprisals, censorship, or ostracism.

While neither of Jamaica's two principal newspapers

printed the critique I made of you at Calabash, and have not carried any subsequent articles about that critique, I choose, perhaps at my own personal risk (and even, as many friends and family have warned and continue to warn me, at the risk of my own life), to believe that Jamaica, unlike many other nations (such as the United States, at times), does not practice censorship. It is that faith, and the pride I carry as someone of Jamaican background, and the desire to share my critique of your words with others, that propels me to write this open letter to you. At the Calabash Festival on that Friday night in May, before I read from my new book, *Our Caribbean: A Gathering of Lesbian and Gay Writing from the Antilles*, I said the following:

> I want to give a special thanks to the Calabash organizers—Colin Channer, Kwame Dawes, and Justine Henzell—for inviting me back to Calabash, this being my second reading at the festival, and for their unceasing generosity to, and support of, writers from around the world. And so, mindful of that generosity and kindness, my conscience will not permit me to begin reading from this book in particular before I say that as a gay man of Jamaican background I am appalled and outraged by the prime minister's having said only three days ago on BBC-TV that homosexuals will not have any place in his cabinet and, implicitly, by extension, in Jamaica.
>
> I guess this means that there will never be any

room in Mr. Golding's cabinet for me and for the many, many other men and women in Jamaica who are homosexual. And so I now feel moved to say directly to Mr. Golding that it is exactly this kind of bigotry and narrow-mindedness that Jamaica does not need any more of, and that you, Mr. Golding, should be ashamed of yourself for providing such an example of how not to lead Jamaica into the future. And so, Mr. Golding, think about how much you are not helping Jamaica the next time you decide to stand up and say that only some Jamaicans—heterosexuals, in this case—have the right to live in their country as full citizens with full human rights, while others—homosexuals—do not. That is not democracy. That is not humane leadership. That is simply the stupidity and cruelty of bigotry.

Although these words received, to my surprise and pleasure, much applause, I remain aware of the grave truth that I could have been killed on the spot, even in the festive Calabash environment in beautiful, quiet Treasure Beach, for speaking them. Yet, as someone who maintains a deep commitment to Jamaica, I had to speak them. With all due respect addressed to your office, Mr. Golding, and at the risk of perhaps getting myself brutally murdered on some future date in Jamaica, I must tell you now that the cruelty and heartlessness of your attitude toward homosexuals does not differ so much from those of your more recent predecessors; any person familiar with Jamaican politics knows that the prime ministers before you had ample opportunities to address the viciousness directed daily toward Jamaican lesbians, gay men, and transgendered people. Those prime ministers, however (I think specifically of P.J. Patterson and Edward Seaga), like you, not only did absolutely nothing to redress this inhumanity, but in fact, by their actions and lack of humanitarian action, aggressively encouraged it: encouraged murder, ostracism, hatred, and ignorance. The ugly fact looms before us, and especially before those of us who are lesbian, gay, bisexual, or transgendered, that you, like those preceding prime ministers, have evidently learned nothing from our violent history in Jamaica—one that goes all the way back to slavery, to the slavery-shadows that stalk us today and that too often move us to continue hating each other and ourselves, as centuries of colonialism and the violence of its oppressions have ensured we do. This state of affairs is without question tragic, but looms as ever more awful in our new century.

In order to more thoroughly convey the enormity of some of this pain, Mr. Golding, I must at this point become slightly more personal. If my throat is sliced open in Jamaica because I am homosexual, or if I am chopped to death with a machete or burned to death in public by a gay-hating group of enraged men and women—entirely likely realities that occur and recur on the island all the time—will you send words of comfort to my aged, ailing mother and all my other relatives? Will you be the one to tell her, as the present leader of her country, that you are sad that her son was so horrendously killed in the land that he loved, but, well, such will always be the fate of Jamaican gay men and lesbians (or, as we are locally and hatefully known, "battymen" and "sodomites")? Will the prime minister's office send my mother flowers as she wonders, half-dead and insane with grief, how the land that bore and raised her could have so cruelly annihilated her son, who dreamt of that land everywhere he traveled? As she wonders how many times the machetes slashed through my flesh before I finally died, will you think of her and remember? Remember that old woman who feared for her son's safety whenever he was in Jamaica, because she, like you and innumerable others, knew the truth—the truth that Jamaica certainly does not love all of its people—"out of many, one," as our national motto states—and certainly not those like me.

There are countless other parents out there like my mother, who fear for their children's safety in Jamaica— the land that they, and some of their children, continue to love in spite of its present agonies. There are many others out there like me who know that we are not only not loved in Jamaica, but in fact are deeply hated by many, throughout every single parish, from Kingston to Mandeville to Montego Bay, to the smallest, dustiest town. Imagine some young child you know having to learn to live on a daily basis with such hatred. Imagine that child struggling to learn, year after year, how, physically and psychically, to survive it.

As you continue to speak harshly against us, as I suspect you will—you will do so because you, like your predecessors, have clearly not yet learned the true horror and awfulness, and the price, of deepest human tragedy—I ask you to remember the violence you are making possible on the bodies and spirits of all these people within and beyond Jamaica. For every single homosexual is, of course, someone's child, brother, sister, grandparent, aunt, uncle, cousin, friend, coworker, teacher, and more. I ask you to remember that young homosexual child in Falmouth, or Oracabessa, or Lawrence Tavern, or Malvern, or Lucea—that child who is utterly vulnerable to the violent future that your thoughtless, inhumane words make more possible. I ask you to think of all those people whose lives your harsh words have made and will continue to make more difficult, more impossible, as your words contribute to the hatred that moves their nightmarish deaths, and mine, closer. I implore you to think of the bitterness (to say the least) and ungodliness that your antigay sentiments and proclamations make a reality, in a country now known internationally—across the entire world—for its murder rate and general violence. I ask you all this, Prime Minister Golding, as your son: for as someone of Jamaican background, I am undeniably your son. No matter how much you may wish to ignore it, there will always be a connection between you and me—a Jamaican connection, certainly, but also the more enduring human one.

As your gay Jamaican son, I ask you, when you next speak against homosexuals anywhere, to remember the blood of this son, and of so many others, that is already on your hands. It is the same blood that stained the hands of your feckless predecessors, and that will yet mark your hands and your memory, whether you know it now or not, for all the years left of your existence. And if indeed I am murdered in Jamaica sometime in the future for being homosexual, please do make sure to tell my mother how sorry—how very sorry—you are, and will always be. She will need to hear it. With my face slashed wide open by a machete and my genitals undoubtedly cut off and shoved down my throat—the way our despised murdered are often found in open gullies and on roadsides, the way too many believed to be homosexual have been discovered in the past—I will not be able to tell her.

Respectfully,
Thomas Glave

"But What Kind of Nonsense Is That?"
Callaloo and Diaspora

===

This recounting begins in my region of the diaspora that is the Caribbean: in Jamaica, in Kingston;
in that wide area north of Kingston proper known as
upper Saint Andrew; in a neighborhood known to me
since the earliest days of my childhood, although in this
recounting I was (I am) a fully grown man: a man like
innumerable others, now sweating and aiming to keep as
still as possible on this late morning of steadily bristling
heat already casting its spite over guango trees, over all
of Kingston Harbour, and over a Blue Mountain peak
shrouded, no doubt to its own relief, in the thick mist
that so often surrounds it and shields it from the spiteful sun: the mist that, when it clears, permits one vision,
from the peak, of Cuba's muscular green lankiness some
ninety miles to the north, and a great deal more on all
sides. Images of diaspora, its smooth flanks; its insistence
that it exists. On this late morning, in the house in upper
Saint Andrew I have known since my earliest days, I am
spending time visiting a relative whom I have not seen
for some time: a relative known for, among other things,
his frequently sharp tongue, who, upon noticing on my
night table my copy of the most recent issue of *Callaloo*
(carried with me on the journey here from the United

States—for as always, I knew that *Callaloo* would never be easy to find for sale in Jamaica), shares the sharpness with me at once, manifested at first in one of the African-isms that have survived in Jamaica—the pronounced suck-ing of teeth—as he exclaims a loud "Eh-eh! *Callaloo*?" (He pronounces it like a true Jamaican, stressing the first syllable.) "Is that really the name of a magazine?" (As he calls it.) "But what kind of nonsense is that?" he snorts, moving on to chase out of the room, my bedroom, three bottle-green hummingbirds that, unnoticed by the both of us, had just darted in, seeking to escape the building heat that would soon lacerate this side of the house un-protected by either mango or guava trees.

"What kind of nonsense"?—but I know what he means. For him, born and raised entirely in Jamaica, "cal-laloo" should and will only ever be that vegetable that is ours and ours alone: distinctly Jamaican, not of or from anyplace or anyone else; not to be mistaken for what Haitians call "callaloo," which would be recognized by people in North America and elsewhere (especially on parts of the African continent) as okra. Not to be mis-taken for what Trinidadians and French Antillean and Brazilian black Bahians consume as an entirely different callaloo. (Diaspora produces singularity but also nation-alism in regard to cuisine and "culture"; diaspora knows the sum of its many parts, but not all the parts acknowl-edge the sum.) Not to be pronounced in any other way, this callaloo, except as we pronounce it, *call*-a-loo; the first syllable rhyming with the Spanish word for salt, *sal*, and the entire word rhyming somewhat with the word "hullabaloo"; and not to be eaten in any way except in the ways we serve it. *That* is callaloo, he thinks, this man who loves to eat and whose form has long betrayed that desire. Not a rassclaat name for a "magazine," he might say, but rather the vegetable hawked loudly by walrus-voiced vendors in open-air markets within Jamaica or in other places: London, Birmingham, Manchester, Toronto, New York, Atlanta, Miami, Los Angeles: anyplace else throughout still another enormous diaspora, the Jamaican one; the green bunches of the vegetable sometimes tied together with blue or beige rubber bands and sold by large-bosomed, generous-buttocked, short-tempered women of all ages in other markets—the same women who will just as soon tell casual browsers and serious shoppers alike not to put one finger pon dem bombo-claat mango as dem woulda tell you fi buy dem callaloo and gwan. (Diaspora creates distinctive language, some-times most vividly expressed in impatience, in rage.) He cannot, this relative of mine, get out of his mind that callaloo: ours, to be sure, but not, as he will refuse to admit, ours alone. On a future night he will dream of how this callaloo must be grasped tightly in the hand on the way home from market, to be dropped off in the kitchen in full view of late-afternoon butterflies and sunset-throated lizards, where it will be soaked in salt water to rid those rubber-veined, tenacious leaves of insects and worms, and later seasoned with pepper and salt and steamed with a little onion; a little skellion and tomato, maybe, and served with anything: white or yellow yam, pumpkin, salt fish and ackee for breakfast;

served with dumpling fried or boiled, green banana and mackerel, or stew chicken. (Diaspora provides necessity, makes possible ample imagination.) That callaloo, I think, remarking his scorn, my head beginning to feel heavy in the encroaching heat; my head beginning to drop forward onto my chest, as the sunset-throated lizards on the ceiling and walls eye me with cautious uncertainty.

Yet, while I had always loved that callaloo—the one that had always so adored the autocratic Jamaican sun, and grown wild throughout the scrubbiest, most unyielding regions of the island and in countless domestic gardens beneath and above the hulking Blue Mountains, and that my parents in New York later grew with exceeding love and care in their immaculately tended garden for inclusion in several of the dishes earlier named—what about the other *Callaloo*?

Yes, the other one: the one with its reliably fat belly, thick spine, and—almost invariably on the front cover—one or another work of immediately arresting art by someone of whom I (often, though not always) might not yet have heard. Art of the diaspora, art about which one has always so fervently wished to learn more. The *Callaloo* that, on this morning of increasingly vengeful heat, watchful lizards, and sun-drugged hummingbirds, reposes on my night table. It is this *Callaloo*—indeed, this *Callaloo*'s entire enormous world—about which my relative knows nothing. He has no idea (nor, in his particular line of work and in the life he leads, does he care to know) what exactly this *Callaloo* has meant to me in the most personal sense, and to all of us in the largest possible sense throughout this sprawling realm we have come to know as and term "diaspora."

"Diaspora, of course," I once argued with someone— a hard-headed man with a long jaw and a tendency, on rainy days, to play grave, slightly scandalous games with his lips. "For *Callaloo* illustrates 'diaspora' in the largest possible sense. But even as it does so, it doesn't just provide information about the diaspora—it *is* the diaspora. In that regard it moves through all of us," I reasoned before his woebegone gaze, wondering what outrageous thing he would next do with his lips. (Rain would descend at any moment.) "All of us," I finished, "and more."

More? But of course. We can recall easily enough the words of Charles H. Rowell, founder and editor of *Callaloo*, in his introduction to his 2002-published anthology *Making* Callaloo: *25 Years of Black Literature*:

When we combine its Brazilian and Caribbean cultural implications, the words *callaloo* and *cararu* become signs for the African diaspora—its cultural mixtures, its racial mélange, its creole peoples . . . I knew none of this when I first named the journal; I only knew that the sound and spelling of the word would attract the attention of North American readers. I did not even think of the obvious: that, like the Trinidadian callaloo, the journal itself was a mixture of forms—and I certainly did not know that the journal would become the site where peoples from all over the African diaspora would speak.[1]

The site, this *Callaloo*, from which the African diaspora's enormity would speak and has spoken time and time again, as in—for a start—the featuring in the journal's pages of creative writers and scholars from places like Curaçao and Aruba and Bonaire, along with writers and painters and scholars from Suriname. For all that work had appeared, hadn't it?—in a special issue on writing and art from the Dutch Antilles and Suriname. At the time, I hadn't yet known about those artists and thinkers when, as a younger man, I opened for the first time *Callaloo*'s broad pages—pages for which I eventually yearned during the months when the journal, its editors busy at their cultural hunting-and-gathering tasks, did not appear. Before receiving with eager hands the special issues on Haitian cultural production, I had not known—no, of course not, even or especially moving through the Anglophone and Hispanophone Caribbean as often as I did, including in those travels the French Caribbean only later—about all the magnificence Haitian art and culture had to offer, had long offered, though not always in English translation from Kreyòl and French; a problem for so many of us in this vast universe we call "the diaspora": the vexation of which work is finally translated into which language, and which is not. (Diaspora reveals the difficulties of diverse languages in concert even as it makes possible, necessary, previously unimagined combinations of concert in language.) And so the work of Yanick Lahens, and Maximilien Laroche, and René Philoctète (whose novel *Massacre River* I finally had the opportunity to teach[2]) first became known to me here, alongside that of Franketienne and Erma Saint-Grégoire and Alix Renaud. *Callaloo*, diaspora, *world*: worlds opened to the willing viewer, as, traveling through the journal, one cannot help but open oneself in return.

"Diaspora"? But wait. For what does it mean, can it mean, that so many of us across this manifold universe we call "diaspora" so often *do not know* about the work others beyond our (often) most immediate knowledge are doing, the artistic and intellectual risks they are taking as they assay new ventures, new ideas, possibilities, identities, combinations of identities (callaloo: make it a stew; mash it up, and wait); new combinations of identities connected to but in *direct contestation of* nationalistic and preconceived—wearily and sometimes smugly received—notions and definitions of "we," as in "*We* have always done it this way"; for "We," if in that sense and terrain centered quite in itself, nonetheless has a right to exist; to exert its imaginative propensities and shape its worlds through its manifold diasporic-mythic elaborations and labyrinthine logics that make sense of the contexts in which, by way of the Middle Passage or some other displacement, it has found itself. For as a diasporic subject, participant, and simultaneous observer, one knows that the knowledge and cultural production of that particular "We"—a subjectivity easily enough transposed, in an historical instant, to the kaleidoscope of one's own—might occur, exist, as aboriginal even while displaced, indigenous while also creolized, callaloo within *Callaloo*: Amerindians and First Nation peoples of North

America, indigenous and displaced—and decimated; Australian aborigines, decimated and displaced; African Americans, arguably the truest "Americans," alongside Native Americans: displaced and reconfigured, though not always with pleasant results: diaspora also discloses tragedy alongside survivors' stunning self-reinvention. All are callaloo and *Callaloo*, and all, across those pages, will always have a place that looms not only as both a literal and figurative place, but also, with consistent import, as a conversation.

But then, toward the furthering of such conversation, *Callaloo*'s very presence and diasporic themes over the years have heightened this vexing question: has our particular "We," wherever we may be, ever taken the time, in the era of the more literal chains' not quite having melted but having somewhat fallen away, to gaze across the water, across the land, in order to witness and comprehend how "They"—those who might bear much resemblance to "We" and might in fact even be a slightly varied form of "We"—do that very (artistic, scholarly) thing at which we believe we excel and which, vis-à-vis our cherished practice and "tradition," we cannot bear to change? ("But what kind of nonsense is that? No, man, you can't do the thing like that." So come to my recollecting ears some words uttered in Jamaica, Barbados; in San Andrés, Colombia, in English and Spanish. Diaspora creates suspicion and insularity, but must, by virtue of its very nature, also knock them apart.) For what does *Callaloo* teach us about black Britain,[3] and black Germany, and black France?—only three examples of still other diasporas also uncovered and explored in the thick, white-paged journal with a (for me) tenacious vegetable as its name.

In partial response to this question, leafing back through the journal's many years, one cannot help but recall particular books, some of whose contents, before the complete book was published, first appeared as articles in *Callaloo*. Books like Brent Hayes Edwards's *The Practice of Diaspora: Literature, Translation, and the Rise of Black Internationalism*; Heike Raphael-Hernandez's collection *Blackening Europe: The African American Presence*; Bennetta Jules-Rosette's *Black Paris: The African Writers' Landscape*; Michel Fabre's *From Harlem to Paris: Black American Writers in France, 1840–1980*; Michelle M. Wright's *Becoming Black: Creating Identity in the African Diaspora*; Hans J. Massaquoi's *Destined to Witness: Growing Up Black in Nazi Germany* (and notice the radical and unfortunate difference between the title of Massaquoi's book in the English translation and the original German: *"Neger, Neger, Schornsteinfeger!" Meine Kindheit in Deutschland*. The German title, with its use of the common racist epithets, acknowledges some of the Nazi ugliness that Massaquoi's book describes in explicit detail); William A. Shack's *Harlem in Montmartre: A Paris Jazz Story between the Great Wars*; Paul Gilroy's *The Black Atlantic: Modernity and Double Consciousness*; Miriam Decosta-Willis's anthology *Daughters of the Diaspora: Afra-Hispanic Writers*; E. Patrick Johnson and Mae G. Henderson's *Black Queer Studies: A Critical Anthology*; Wendy W. Walters's *At Home in Diaspora: Black International Writing*; Gordon Heath's

Deep Are the Roots: Memoirs of a Black Expatriate; and so many other works that, in innumerable ways, speak out of both *Callaloo* and callaloo, and resound back to *Callaloo*. It wouldn't be an exaggeration to state that *Callaloo*'s presence and substance, since its very beginning, have helped to foster the sterling intellectual work and recovery/memory projects of texts like these that now, more than ever, exemplify an increasing preoccupation of scholars, thinkers, and artists across the globe with the nonmonolithic entity we term "diaspora," what exactly "diaspora" constitutes even as it morphs and expands (and sometimes turns back on itself, surprising itself and its inhabitants)—a preoccupation that displays increasing awareness of the inappropriateness of reductive and essentialist thinking in regard to the sprawling entity: diaspora, a restless creature-creation of history, imagination, violence, and desire, that, whether we like it or not, remains always protean and mercurial, to say the least. The scholars and artists whose visions populate *Callaloo*'s pages have revealed, perhaps sometimes to their own astonishment, the multifold ways in which, aware of it or not, untold numbers of us, like steadfast jazz musicians, have improvised unpredictable notes both mellifluous and discordant . . . all of them, like each of us in the diaspora and beyond, in conversation with each other.

Did *Callaloo* do this for me? Did it open up my way of thinking about this thing we call "diaspora" even as I yearned to stake my particular Jamaican American territorial claim in it? Yes, I think so. Absolutely. For the very existence of this thick-spined journal inspires one like me, like all of us, to begin thinking more deeply about (for example) black Canadians: not only those in Toronto who, beneath scarlet maple leaves, haggle over the price of callaloo in that ruthlessly tidy city's epic markets, but also those in Halifax, Saskatoon, Winnipeg, St. John's: how they live, who they are, how they think, how they write and paint and draw and sculpt, how they dance, how they make music, and how they will yet be—for they, like so many others, will yet be. In regions of snowy wastes made more hospitable by the scent of dasheen and callaloo warmed in certain kitchens, black Canadian writers intone the fluttering languages of itinerant birds: Dionne Brand, H. Nigel Thomas, André Alexis, Nalo Hopkinson, Esi Edugyan, Pamela Mordecai, George Elliott Clarke, Lawrence Hill. And more, in the increasing callaloo of black Canadian anthologies that call and respond in sea-washed dreams to the journal with a tenacious vegetable for its name.

"A network center," I insisted in conversation with a woman given to teal and lavender dreams and an obsession with the elephants she had not yet glimpsed on so many trips to the continent where life on the planet, migrating from the vast waters, began. "This *Callaloo*. It's a—"

"Yes," she interrupted, "I know. It's a place of convergence."

And there, I thought: she did it. Provided me with the language I needed. With the word. *Convergence.* The place where, more than ever before, Latin American blackness (thinking especially of cultural production by

Latin American peoples of African descent, so frequently overlooked or ignored even by those who ought to know better) is provided a place: the multiplicities in literature, visual art, and culture of Veracruz, of Cuba; the more and more and more and *more* of gargantuan Brazil, el "gigante" del cantante cubano Pablo Milanés. Here, in the accumulation of pages that comprise the fat belly held in place by the thick spine, the scholars speak to the artists speaking to the scholars who respond in Spanish, in Portuguese; here, where, in the largest possible sense but also in the most invariably specific, we see ourselves and distillations of the worlds that make ourselves: "We" in the callaloo of faces and the work produced by so many image- and word- (and in the case of Milanés and others, music-) producing hands. For so it is that the journal that links its name to a tenacious vegetable (or a soup, or stew) insists that we do.

Insists that we do as its contents demand, more consistently, that this universe many term "diaspora" must move beyond African America—interrogating the very use, often blithe and assuming, of the word "America," while remembering that all those in "American" countries are "Americans," untold numbers of them constituting part of the sprawling diasporic entity.[4] For "blackness," callaloo and *Callaloo* have illustrated, is not and cannot be—should not be—imaginatively or otherwise confined to Mississippi or Alabama, New York or New Orleans, Chicago or Los Angeles, Baltimore or Philadelphia. Or Savannah. Or Atlanta. Or Dallas, St. Louis, Milwaukee, or Oakland. The creature named "diaspora" might not even entirely be—indeed, cannot be—"black" as the idea of "blackness" is popularly understood (and often unthinkingly accepted by, and propounded by) many in the United States; for what about the realities of creolization and syncretism applicable to the Amerindians of South and Central America and to black Europeans—creolization and syncretism discussed in, for example, some of the texts earlier mentioned? They are here, they are (t)here. And so, uncertain of itself and completely sure of itself, the "We" of our present and past grows larger, bolder, and more generous.

On that distant afternoon in Kingston, however, I do not yet know any of this. The afternoon remains a sequence of somnolent hours thick with the scents of powerfully ripening guava, and chicken jerked in heavy oil drums by bearded, wool-capped men (wool-capped in spite of the blistering heat) out on the road increasingly noisy with the afternoon's growing traffic. A sequence of hours in which I, heavy-lidded, lethargic as only the Caribbean's imperious sun can make me, soon fall into a deep sleep, in which, after but a few moments, I meander, insubstantial, beneath a descending cloud of magenta butterflies intent on chewing their way through a patch of healthy-with-life callaloo. As the sun and moon rise and set here with an eye only toward their own interests, so time chooses once again to scoff just now at Western fixations on "time," and all at once rushes without warning toward the future moment when those same butterflies, pursued by half-chewed callaloo stalks, plummet from the sky in an unending rain that will darken that dream-sky and relent only when (gasping, with a taste in my mouth of sleep's inexplicable vengeances on the unwary living) I struggle back to waking. A rain shower did fall while I so briefly dreamt, bringing a blessing of cooling in its silver; but keeping in mind that all the Antilles (and perhaps Jamaica in particular) can spring large surprises, I'm relieved to find that the rain was merely rain as usual, carrying with it only the hundreds of orchid petals that managed to blossom, as some species are inclined to do, out of our view so high, *high* up among the clouds in that ever-spreading sky. My eyes still heavy with sleep, I turn to the night table on which the issue of *Callaloo* I brought with me had rested. It is there still—its belly heavy as always, its spine reliably thick. I take it into my hands, hold it, and, closing my eyes once again, dream briefly of a man, or many men, and women, and people both male and female, pounding a drum that tells a story the content of which I am certain I had sometime known, but cannot, in this moment between drifting, waking, and the aftermath of the orchid-filled sighing rain, exactly recall.

In a few minutes, my relative will poke his head into the bedroom to announce tartly that we will have callaloo with salt fish, ackee, bammy, and boiled dumplings for breakfast tomorrow. "And *that*," he will say, "will be the only type of callaloo we are going to deal with in this house." Smiling faintly and making no reply to him as he walks off with a loud suck of his teeth, I will open the pages of this *Callaloo*, and begin to read. Something in those pages on women writers from Puerto Rico this time . . . Puerto Rico, out there across the water to the east, and in the pages that continue to speak across the continents, illuminating the depth and breadth and history of the continents; in innumerable instances, depths and breadths and histories many would prefer still remain undisclosed, untold. The pages that I will have perhaps finished reading by the time we breakfast on the other callaloo tomorrow morning, even as I recall this afternoon of silver rain laced with sighing orchid blossoms and the scent of jerked chicken wafting in from a busy road. The pages that—at least today, this afternoon—do not yet plummet from the sky in the company of ravenous magenta butterflies, so many of them, as silver rain again begins to fall, whispering its ancient memories over those ripening guavas and mangoes just beyond my window. (In diaspora all things are possible, so many things yet remain unseen.) The pages that conjure and comprise this *Callaloo*, I think, drifting toward dreams once again. Yes, this *Callaloo*, so many voices echo and respond. Fat-bellied, they say. Thick-spined. This one.

Toward a Queer Prayer

Today, or on another day perhaps not so different from this one—a day of light and birds and even laughter, genuine laughter—another faggot in Jamaica will perhaps scream, or not, as someone moves to burn down his home with him inside it; or tries to rip open his bowels with a machete, as he, that faggot (picture his watching eyes, watching; picture his open or just-closed mouth, sometimes waiting) is perhaps momentarily distracted by looking at the sea, at our gorgeous bluegreen Caribbean Sea. He, the faggot, pondering waves there; pondering color and light and birds, and for possibly more than this moment, not dwelling—no, not at all—on how much his body and his flesh, and his very breath, are all still so hated, hated, *hated* in Jamaica. For this moment, as he ponders that beckoning water into which scores of his enslaved ancestors leapt off ships to their deaths three hundred years before, he *un*remembers the fact that this country, for the most part, has never loved him; that its motto of "Out of many, one people" seems, astonishingly, not ever—not even after death—to include him; and that in fact, one of the nation's proudest patriots, in the name of God and nation, or simply in the spirit of fear and outrage, might, even on this day of light and birds and color, already be dreaming either of eviscerating him

or burning him alive, or both. Such dreams of annihilation that occasionally lead to fearsome acts should come
as no surprise in the Jamaica many of us know and love
in spite of itself: the country that we know and love in
spite of the fact that this Jamaica, the same one that ven-
omously calls some of its male citizens faggots or battymen, and calls some of its female and male citizens
sodomites, would just as soon slice open faggots' throats
as see them—me, us—hanged from someone's mango
tree. It should come as no surprise that somewhere, on a
day not so different from this one, some "lesbian bitch"
(as one has sometimes heard *those people* referred to in
Jamaica), or a woman perceived to be a lesbian, is raped
and perhaps murdered, maybe eviscerated: yes, for that is
what she deserves, isn't it? Because a woman should be a
woman, goddamnit, and not aim to be like a rassclaat man,
no true? She, the bitch, should know her damnblasted place,
no true? Know her place even though some of us say that
we are not, in Jamaica, like South Africa: we do not have
"corrective rape" here. We are not ignorant and dirty like
those whom some of us would consider disgusting black
Africans, even though many of us, if not most, are also
black. And lesbian bitches and faggots in Jamaica should
know their place because this kind of carrying on, this
faggotness and lesbian-ness and simple filthy perversion,
is pure wickedness, nastiness, filthiness. It is an *abomination*
(so it has been said). It is a sickness, a white people t'ing, a
(to some, to many) satanic t'ing . . . a t'ing we cannot bear
inna dis ya country, Massa God: so *annihilate* de battyman
dem, de sodomite dem. So many have indeed thought

and on occasion shouted; and so many have believed and believe still: yes, by God, by Jesus His son on the cross, it must be done. And if at least some of the nasty people are annihilated or exorcised (or both), and if enough eyes and backs are turned away when the police or others torture them, people will dance and cheer and sing in the streets, won't they? Many people will, won't they? Yes, of course: for isn't that what some people did when, not so many years ago now, one of Jamaica's most famous faggots, and one who helped to found that nastyman organization, the Jamaica Forum for Lesbians, All-Sexuals, and Gays (J-FLAG), was killed? Brian Williamson. Chopped up with a machete, someone chopped him; carved up with an ice pick, someone carved him. Brian: remember him? His insides were ripped open by metal gripped in a pair of angry hands. Upon announcement of his death that June 2004 morning, people who happened to be out on the road where he lived began dancing, dancing in that narrow New Kingston road: dancing for joy outside Brian's home at 3A Haughton Avenue, as his still-warm corpse was carried out of his house by those whose work it is to do such things. And many people who were watching on that lovely day not unlike this one danced and even sang the song, that so-infamous song, the annihilation anthem by Buju Banton: *Boom bye bye inna batty bwoy head / Rude bwoy no promote the nasty man, dem haffi dead.*[1]

Because that is what we deserve, many people in Jamaica still believe. Because that is what faggots are, many people in Jamaica (and throughout the world) still believe. Unpersons. Not-people. *Things.*

Pedophiles. Aberrations. The depraved things called faggots. Lesbian bitches. Battymen. Sodomites.

And all of it—blood, words, dancing—evidence of the great harm that the denial of full human citizenship does to human beings. Denial of the human citizenship that makes people into ghosts, unpeople, *things. Things* which, because less than human, are more easily hated, feared, despised. And killed.

And so perhaps, all those years ago, the small group of us who founded J-FLAG had already had enough of our thing-ness, or had decided to pay it no attention and move on. Perhaps we had had enough of faggots' body parts tossed into ravines for mangy dogs to sniff and consume, and policemen's batons cracked into our skulls either before or after those batons had been shoved up our asses, then down our throats. Perhaps we decided that it might be better to face head-on the possibility of being chopped up, instead of living always in fear of being chopped up. I remember that one of us, who departed the group soon after our first meeting, asked us with great concern, in regard to the danger of the work to come: "But if you were a Jew in Nazi Germany, would you go about stating loudly that you were a Jew?" That was the exact question, and so many years later I can still see his face, staring, wondering. None of us could say what Jews *would* have done. And however one felt about his question, the fact that he had felt the emotion that had motivated it was significant. I replied, "But what else can we do? What else is there to do, now?" And so impossibly, possibly, we went forth, and went forth again, and all these years later, although the founding group has dispersed, the organization lives on, and only one of the founders—Brian—has been murdered. And many more lesbians and gay men, and some transgendered people, have found in J-FLAG a place in Jamaica that they can call "home," of a kind; a place that they can call their own; a place where, on a day not so different from this one, or one exactly like it, they can sit down, recalling at some point the beauty of our gorgeous bluegreen Caribbean, and actually touch the miracle of their own living flesh, and say, or think, *But yes. I exist. I'm alive, here, and that is a good thing. Alive, here, where, at least for now, no one will try to toss acid upon me, or spit in my face and call me an abomination, or cut off my hands and hate me because in me they see nothing but filth, just sickening filth. Not here, where I can be alive. Where I can have flesh, a face, and my own hands.*

And Jamaica? It has had to contend with us. Is contending. Contending even though—for the moment—it has rarely seen our faces. For to show our faces without great caution in Jamaica, even now—perhaps especially now—just might bring death in some quarters, in many quarters; just might bring fire and kerosene and machetes, and then people dancing on a road somewhere. But Jamaica knows, more than ever now, that we are *here*. It knows, more than ever now, our beloved but often cruel country, that it may kill some of us, but by no means all. It cannot murder all of the women; it cannot annihilate every single man. The prime minister knows it, Jamaica's parliament knows it. Fire and machetes, but also resistance. *Resistance.* Everyone knows it.

Ultimately, perhaps I really wanted to help form J-FLAG because of him: because of that little faggot, sitting there, broken-fingered and partly burned, in a dark corner of my most lonely, most intimate imagination. A corner of exile and sometimes death. Sitting there, that little mincing, lisping, despicable faggot who should have been shot dead in his youth; who should have been raped, who was raped; who should have been beaten, and was beaten, constantly: that sickening little faggot, with the too-large eyes and the swaying hips, who might have been me or so many others; who was me, and is, and will be many others. It is for him, and for all the others—the women, the men, the mannish women and the womanish men and all those yet to come—that, I am sure, we walked toward great fear and uncertainty, but also toward the power of freedom and liberation. There is something in the pursuit of liberation that feels exactly like—that *is*—prayer. Let these words, then, and a part of this day, become a kind of prayer for all of them—for us—and also for the dead. A prayer with open hands and heart offered up for the living and the dead. A prayer that already knows that the time is coming, will come, when a faggot or sodomite might walk alongside our beautiful Caribbean, thinking of nothing, nothing whatsoever, but water, waves. Silence. Someone who, just walking, on a day not so different from this one, will gradually turn his or her face up to the sky and think, *But yes. Here. Alive. Where I am. Where I can be. Alive.*

THE BLOODPEOPLE IN THE LANGUAGE

A nd even now being in Jamaica and writing this and knowing that I am writing these words thinking about death and the end of all things and the loss of everything—for loss has indeed recently come very near; has knocked, made itself felt, known, present. And thinking about it, loss, death, so much because there has been so much death in this family, my family, recently, so much: the death of a cousin, a fundamentalist born-again Christian who committed suicide not long ago by firing a gun into his chest after losing custody of his sons in an acrimonious divorce case and also discovering that one of those sons was not his own, his biological own (though very much his spiritual own, the child who had always known only him as, and called him, "Daddy")—the child not his biologically but, as he learned to his evident devastation, his best friend's. Then another cousin who died only weeks ago and completely unexpectedly; and that cousin's sister-in-law who died after a brief time in a coma, and so young, so very young, only in her thirties; and then my beloved and favorite aunt thinking that she was going to die and suffering a profound mortality crisis upon pondering the very real proximity of her own death, who as of this writing lies slowly dying in a Northeast Bronx hospice.[1] And then most recently my always-vibrant and impossible and sometimes viciously cruel, sometimes deeply loving mother, who at eighty-seven years of age in the spring of 2011 suffered a stroke, a massive stroke, people told me over the phone: my mother lying on a bed without speech and without mobility on her right side, first in a hospital, then in an "acute rehabilitative facility," and then in a "subacute rehabilitative facility," regaining speech though slowly, painfully, with great difficulty, and still no sign of any significant restored mobility. And then remembering my sister, my only sibling, dead these many years from breast cancer at the age of forty-one. It was not right, such a death can never be right for anyone. It was not right for her children who were teenagers at the time; not right for her husband who, though I have never at all really cared for him, and in fact for very good reasons have often despised and utterly loathed him and loathe him still, I know loved her beyond imagining. And it was not right, that death, for my mother, who herself proceeded into an unfathomable tailspin after her daughter's death—the daughter who, in fact and very unfortunately, she had physically and emotionally abused and tormented for years, unmercifully, alternating that cruelty with genuine love, or what she had perceived to be love, in the deeply twisted way some people perceive and define love. And then four years before my sister's death, the death of my father: my father whom I had without question worshipped and adored for all of his life, for all of the years I had known him, even as I later came to scorn him at times, and even to repudiate him, as surly rebellious teenagers are often known to do with parents, at least in the contemporary West. My father, beloved, idolized: a gray-headed man who was born to garden, blessed with intuitive understanding of the soil and green things. My father who, like so many Jamaicans and especially those raised "in country," in a small farming community in deep central Jamaica, loved his garden, and died in a hospital at the age of seventy-two when I was still quite young, after whose death ("after the first death, there is no other," the poet wrote—but he was wrong, so very wrong) I immediately lost all sense of time and place and purpose and even being, by which I mean my own being—for what could be the point of *being* after something like that? Who would wish to *be*, to be alive still, to breathe and walk upon the blessed gorgeous earth, this planet so miraculous and life-sustaining (but also life-taking), after something like that? He died. They all died. But his death especially, his leaving this planet especially, his departing with a gasp in the last spasms of cardiac arrest and physical expiration in that cold clean sterile machine-filled hospital room in the Northeast Bronx, was cataclysm. Indefinable. Irrevocable. The unquestionable and utterly ultimate and terrible, *awful* ending of all things, I believed at the time; in that time, that awful very dark time, during which I wished during the *very* empty—actually hollow, and strangely soundless, feelingless, sensationless—chilly days and nights and weeks that followed only to lie in a dark room for days and cease to be, just cease to be—*let it all end now*, my limp body had thought (my body in that time thinking because my mind, shattered or simply shut

down somehow throughout those endless airless moments quite unable to think)—so my body had thought
in that protecting dark dank room in the basement of my
parents' house, where, across a dirty, rumpled sheet on a
caving-in mattress, my body had thought, *if I can just stay
here for the rest of my life I will be fine, just fine*: my mind
filled with (filled with? Or, more accurately, possessed
by?) the strangeness and stupidity and outrage and blank-
ness of grief. Too much death in what was and remains
for me the inescapably personal realm: a lot of death,
through which, in moments of clarity and compassion
and human caring, makes me want to feel and feel and
know the sorrow and grieving and agony of all those in
all the villages across the world who have been incinerated, who have been firebombed, who have been bayoneted, who have been machine-gunned, where nearly
(or all) of the women and children, and many of the
men, have been raped, then raped again, and where the
old people have been knocked senseless to the ground
and trod upon by soldiers' or mercenaries' bootsteps, and
intestines from those of all ages have been left out to
dry in the hot, the *very* hot, sun. The grief of one, the
grief of another: even (especially) in the midst of my
own much smaller grief I wish not to forget them. I will
never forget them, faceless though the world at large often wants them to be, and small though my grief actually
is or would appear to some alongside the (in some cases)
centuries-long shadows of theirs.

And so even now I am here in Jamaica where in the

language, the daily and nightly language and voices, I hear them all: hear those close to me who have died or who are dying. Those who are leaving, who have left. I continue to hear all of them in the patois, the creole, the cadences, the words, the intonations, the sounds, the expressions, the proverbs, the syntax, the utterances of *Yes, my dear* and *Massa God, do* and *But see ya?* and *Mi cyaan believe seh* and *Ah mi one know seh him woulda drop lick pon har* and more, so much more: here in Jamaica at this time partly because *this, this is what I must have,* I think: this, the primal language of my existence and being that, for me, conjures them, the living and the dead. Conjures and summons memory. Language that is memory. That is recollection. For aside from the profound love that I feel, *feel* for this country that yet cannot love me because of who I am and how I love and desire and exist—and in spite of and also alongside the fury that I feel for this country that cannot love me or sometimes even see me because of who I am and how I love and desire—it is here where I most often wish to be, and must be, so that—in part—I might hear and feel and walk through the language that conjures all of them, those no longer here and those here for perhaps not much longer: here, parents and family, who, though I may sometimes hate them, though I may hate them and love them, I nonetheless hear them in the language that conjures their presences and beings once again *so that they are not dead they do not feel dead*; so that hearing them, I feel more safe—perhaps what can only be an illusory feeling of safety from complete aloneness and finally mortality—than I have ever felt anyplace else:

here, on this island where those more inclined to violence and hatred would (at the least) scorn or avoid me, and at the most do far worse; far worse such as kill me, of course. Here, on an island that, in these years of intensified crime, violence beyond belief, is in no way safe. Jamaica. This place of the language. This place that is home but that, like "home" itself, is uneasy; that offers often unsafe, often deceptively welcoming arms.

And so in hearing the language here and feeling all of them in the cadences I am returned to—I am *in*—the most core part of myself (so I believe) and my past: a past which one would often rather not remember or think about, especially the more distant historical one. Here among my people, my insufferable and hateful and loving and deeply beloved people, where I hear the parents and their parents and all of them going further back in time than I can possibly imagine; and so in moments of deepest loneliness and longing (my sister should not have died so young; my father should not have died at all; my mother, spiteful and cruel and loving as she has been and even in the midst of her stroke still is, should not die at all, though her dying would, I have often thought, be to me an absolute relief, an absolution, deliverance), the language of daily living comforts and assuages. It assures me, even if the assurance is only an illusion that I not only accept but grasp in unabashed desperation: the desperate belief that there is and must be some consistency, some possibility—the raw possibility of going on, continuing—in the radical adventure known more often as life; the vastly unpredictable arena known as life. Life most definitely not everlasting. Here, watching the distant mango trees respond with what looks like lilting pleasure to the evening breeze's caress, I hear them. Feel them. I know that they, those people, are here, contradictory as the feelings about them will be and are. It remains unfathomable to some non-Jamaican friends how much I adore this country and its complicated, exasperating people who, over centuries, fashioned a brilliant, acrobatic language—one well familiar with harsh and more gentle irony—out of unspeakable suffering, but also out of the miracle of (against so many odds) survival.

It is something to know that you so dearly and even desperately love a country in which you know that you are not, in fact, safe, no matter the seductiveness of your illusions; no matter your desire for safety (actual safety itself, whatever it actually is and wherever one finds it, being finally perhaps simply the assurance of love), or for faith. Such love (or faith, or desire) is not quite a choice. It is simply a way of being, foolhardy in this context, perhaps; a way of being that beats insistently through your pathetic vulnerable heart and is, simply, somehow enduringly *there*. It is something to know that the place that provides you with such indescribable joy in your heart—yes, in your very deepest heart, upon arriving in it in the present day at the same airport where you arrived in it as a child over and over again and where, far beyond that airport, in the hills of cooler, greener upper Saint Andrew, you spent time as a child—is a place that, no matter how much you love it, you know could destroy you; as, indeed, could several other places. For where, finally, is "safety"? I have never quite fully known. Only a very stupid or self-deceiving black man, and in my case also a homosexual with clearly not-white skin, living in the United States (or in many other places) would believe that he is in any way "safe." What we can know is that "safety" is, in this deeply fraught world, as elusive as shadows at dusk: glimpsed for a moment, then gone; then maybe returned at some future point, but not, I suspect, for long. Some children, often the most vulnerable among us, know this; some people in besieged places, whether nation or domestic sphere, seeking safety for themselves and their children, know this. In my smaller circumstances, I can hope that some kind of safety resides perhaps in particular memories; perhaps in language that brings back both substance and occasionally remembered form and flesh of those both living and dead.

(But then for a moment, with great happiness, indeed even joy, I remember Denver's conversation with her deceased grandmother Baby Suggs in *Beloved*: Denver, the at-her-wit's-end daughter and granddaughter fighting to save both her mother Sethe and herself from "the nastiness of life and the meanness of the dead," rescued and heartened—emboldened—by the sudden, unexpected voice in her ear of one long-dead black woman—the heart and prize of connection:

"You mean I never told you nothing about Carolina? About your daddy? You don't remember nothing about how come I walk the way I do and about your mother's feet, not to speak of her back? I never told you all that? Is that why you can't walk down the steps? My Jesus my."

But you said there was no defense.

"There ain't."

Then what do I do?

"Know it, and go on out the yard. Go on."[2])

If people with whom you are close have begun to die or sicken to some extent, the dying or sickening occasioning in you feelings of longing and loneliness (and also fear), and if you are me or someone like me, like so many of us—you might begin to court the dead; to have conversations, and then maybe longer conversations, with the dead. (If you are the descendant of African slaves, as I am and as so many of us are, this is something that you may not be able to do without eventually losing your mind, acknowledging the enormity of the history and experience; if you are the descendant of African slaves, as so many of us are and as I am, you will know that, acknowledging the enormity of that history and experience, this is eventually something that you will probably have to do, hopefully without risk of losing your mind. *Peace*, and *ancestors*, you might think, as I have often thought; for in the journey of engaging with the dead you must, I have learned and still am learning, move yourself toward some conceptualization of peace, however defined, and some squaring with ancestors, which, paradoxically, given one's history as a person of African descent, may bring anything but peace.) You feel them around you, sometimes those ancestral dead; you know that they are there. Of course you hear them in the daily Jamaican language that brings them back to you. But you also dream of them, ruminate about them, wonder what (for those whom you did not actually know) their faces looked like. You wonder even what the face of your paternal great-great-grandfather Stephen Sharp Glave looked like: a white man born in Lythe, North Riding, Yorkshire, England, who emigrated to Jamaica from England in the early nineteenth century and died there, in Manchester, in 1873, and whose gravestone you saw not far from the town of Mile Gully, in the churchyard of the now de-consecrated, supposedly haunted Anglican church ("the duppy church"). That had originally been St. George's Church, where, in the late nineteenth century, Stephen served on the church committee and at some point also as one of the church's wardens. (And it was very moving, you remember, and deeply strange, to see your surname on a worn, weatherbeaten nineteenth-century grave-stone . . . knowing that, in addition to sharing that name, some DNA of the man buried in that ground moved in the present through your living body.) You wonder about the "brown" woman, Catherine "Kitty" Wright—your paternal great-great-grandmother. Was her grave-stone among those more unreadable in the weed-choked churchyard? Where did her bones lie—the bones of the woman whom Stephen did not marry and who bore him several children, among them an earlier Thomas Glave. (The very accurate family genealogy shows that there had already been several Thomases in the Glave line, going as far back as the 1740s in England.) Stephen and Kitty's son Thomas was your great-grandfather, born in 1839 in Whitby, Manchester, and deceased there in 1901: the Thomas who fathered your grandfather, Caleb Glave, and the Thomas for whom your father, that Thomas's grandson, was presumably named.

But then who was that brown woman, Catherine "Kitty," whom Stephen Sharp Glave, for whatever reasons, did not marry, though she obviously shared his bed? (Or at least bore him children.) How did she live? How did she live, Catherine the great-great-grandmother, her skin marking her in the postslave colony as most definitely not white, a person virtually without rights or claim of her own? A woman-ancestor who had lived through the late slave era in Jamaica and into the time of Emancipation? How did she live with and bear children for a man who stipulated in his will that, as we have known definitively since the early years of this century, any of his children who married a "Black Person" would be disinherited?[3] (He made good on this threat with one of his progeny, leaving her only a mule. A resounding brava! to that daughter, one Maria Glave, who, born in Whitby, Manchester, in 1840, married one [evidently black] Lionel deSilva Henriques, thus daring to buck her intransigent and, as we would say in this "modern" century, bigoted father.) How did she live, how did she die? I would like to know her face and her voice, and the sound of her nineteenth-century brownwoman Jamaican language. I would like to know her life, as much as

I would like to know that of the man whose property, in a sense, she became after Emancipation: the lives of these great-great-grandparents and the lives of all those who followed, as much as I would like to know the lives and faces and voices of all the Thomas Glaves who preceded me over the past two hundred and fifty years, and others. They are there, in my imagination and historical memory; they are most definitely there.

At certain times—times like this one, when your mother has recently had a massive stroke and you are feeling extremely overwhelmed and very alone, alone and often really frightened—frightened when you wonder what will happen next, what *can* happen next, and how you will get through all of it without actually losing your mind (but then thank God for prayer, and for open night skies and stars and memories of warm Caribbean water and whispering trees. Thank God for quietness, and the possibility of prayer)—at times like this, you do wish very much, yearn very much, for a brother. An older brother. An experienced one. One who, in the face of trials and great anxiety, would always, invariably, be confident. That brother. The one who, like your dead sister, would seem always to know everything. The one who would always have a reasonable (if sometimes acerbic, even unkind and condescending, as was often the case with her) response for everything; the one who, if he actually existed, would surely, in this idealistic imagining, have broad shoulders to rely upon, and a deep resonant voice to match the frequent smile on his face: the smile that, like the calming assurance in his so-confident voice, would have said to you on numerous occasions, without being authoritarian and with steadfast good humor, *Yes. Yeah man*, as a Jamaican would say. *All right, then. Don't worry. No bodda worry.* That one: the brother about whom you have often dreamt. An older brother (although a younger one would be welcome) of whom, as you listen hungrily to the sounds of your parents and other bloodpeople in the daily Jamaican language, and hear them, you would ask, *And so how is Mother doing today? Did you visit her? Does she seem depressed? Is she responding to the speech therapy? Is she forming entire sentences yet? Are they actually giving her antianxiety medication? Is she making any friends there? Will you go to the "facility" today, or tomorrow? Should I go there today, or tomorrow? How are you holding up? You know that I love you, don't you? And oh yes*, you would tell him, that brother, *remember that: remember how much, how very much I love you. How much I love you dearly, and how we will, we* will *get through this together, brother. Yes, of course we will: because the older people will die, and some of the younger people may die also, as our sister did, and as we—who knows, who can possibly know?—may die sooner than we think; but we* will, *beloved brother whose voice and presence I also hear in the language, we* will *get through it all. Trust me on that one. Believe me. All right.*

But he, that beloved but imagined and fictitious brother about whom you have dreamt and for whom you have yearned for years upon years since (if not before) your sister's untimely death, does not breathe air, at least not the air of this planet. And so because he does not exist and has never existed, you know, *know*, that you will have to move through this landscape alone. Move at times with the support of friends, who are loving, yes; but whom you know also do—as they should—have their own lives, their own responsibilities; as he, your imagined brother, no doubt would have had his own. But responsibilities and life of his own though he would have had, he would have been one of your bloodpeople—and hopefully one of the kind ones, unlike those in Jamaica not pleased with your most profound pleasure and yearning, with your longings for other men. Ideally, whatever your imagined brother's erotic inclinations, he would not have reacted to you in as cold a manner as many of the other bloodpeople have done. Ideally, you and he would not have been enemies, not irritable and sarcastic in each other's presence, but friends—dear friends. But you do not have a brother who is either a friend or an enemy, except in the place for which, at times like this one, with your mother lying in a "facility" because of a stroke that has reduced her to an invalid, you are deeply grateful: your imagination.

And when you are in Jamaica as you are now, listening for your living and many dead bloodpeople in the language and seeking to conjure them, conjure them and bring them all around you—for this is partly a search against loneliness, partly a quest for companionship and the belief that you are, in truth, very loved, partly because you wish so much to give love—you also think: and yes, would it not be wonderful, I mean truly wonderful, to have someone to love just now? Someone against whose smooth body you could press your own for an evening after time at the "facility," in an hour when you feel very close to, or actually possessed by, tears; someone about whom you could wrap your arms and whose arms would wrap about you, holding you like that, like *that*: pressing his face against yours and all of himself against all of you; in the darkness that would be the darkness preceding far less agonizing dreams, saying things very quietly, like, *Oh, but you know, it's really going to be all right.* He would, for sure, say things like that. *But really?* you would respond, silently apologizing for the warm saltiness on your face, the saltiness that he would taste and taste many times again. *Yes*, he would say, doing that—what he always had enjoyed doing to you—and then doing it again to your eyelids and to your mouth, your eyelashes, and all the parts of you that he would, rest assured, know by heart. *It really will be*, he would say, pulling your face against his, and then perhaps holding it on his chest. Holding. *And God, yes*, you would think, *how good his hands feel. How like prayer and absolution itself his hands feel. I am loved*, you would think, *and love him. And so by God above and all around, in spite of this grief, in spite of this pounding and scratching in my chest from watching my mother shrink in her own disabled and disabling agony, love—love!—actually is possible.*

But of course, he would say again, *it really will be. Will be all right.* He would say that even though you would of course know and suspect that, as smart as he is, as sensitive and compassionate and honest as he is, he really does know, as do you, that it will in fact not be at all all right. It will in no way ever again be all right. How can it be all right? you would not ask him. How can it possibly be all right when after all this time she, your mother, is still there in the "facility" and it has now begun to look as though she will never regain full speech or full mobility, never leave the wheelchair in which you have always seen her over these months, and thus, it is clear, possibly never be able to return to her own home to live out her very old years with the cat she adores and the garden without which, it always seemed, she could not live for long? Or, at least, if she returns there, she will not return as the ambulatory and powerfully energetic person, even in her late eighties, she had previously been. How can it in any way be all right when she becomes more and more depressed and devastated each day when she cannot form her words, can barely form entire sentences, and spends so much time both when you visit and when she is alone crying and screaming, perhaps thinking things like *Where is my life, what has happened to my life?* All right? How can any of it really be all right? you would not ever ask him. But then you would know that the mere fact that he said it was enough, in those moments in darkness before the advance of less agonizing dreams (more agonizing when you are alone). It would be enough for you to know then in that shared darkness why, yes, *why* you had always loved him so much. *Because yes how lucky I am to have you and to love you and to feel you holding me like this*, you would think, saltiness on your face and his face against yours and those arms so *about* you, *holding* you, and yours about him. It would be then that you would know that there are times, maybe many times, when people do not have to tell you the truth, the absolute truth, in order for you to love them and for them to love you. There are times when life actually can be possible in spite of the absence of ultimate absolute truth; times when lies, utter lies, can make you smile—or at least can make it possible for you to open your eyes in a dark room and look at someone, really *look* at him, and think, know, that jumping off a building or cutting your wrists (ideas which have, even if briefly, flashed through your head these past weeks) is really not the best way to do things; that there really is a way to do things, even with, or especially with, lies—a way, ways, that can be noble, bracing, embracing, even brave—and very necessary. But, like the brother of your most primal and reaching dreams, he, that wonderful man who would hold you and press your face into his as he whispered, *All right, it will be, now try to sleep*, does not exist. It is possible that you will listen for his voice and presence in the language also—in a language, that is, that might finally be a different one entirely from any language you have ever inhabited or known.

Once, once upon a time—

Once upon a realm, in a far-off kingdom by the sea, there lived a small boy who believed that his elder sister knew everything. He believed that she knew the names and historical categories of snails (which she did), and the infinite personalities of trees (patient, impatient, skulking, among them), and how mustard leaves crept and crawled—crawled, and even walked—until taller plants could no longer ignore them, had to engage with them; and exactly what the ancient order of rainbows—rainbows well-known and those more elusive, that sometimes nourished secretive, determined sea creatures—have to do with words like *homunculus*, with words like *crepuscular* and even *adamantine*; with notions like *space, consume*, and *unrendered*. He knew that she, his elder sister, stood approximately seven feet tall when measured with bamboo yardsticks, and slightly taller when measured with those made of cane. He imagined, that boy (and in truth he could be at times a rather silly, fanciful child), that he would one day grow old with her—foolish child, can you imagine?—and that they would talk about things as old people. Talk about things like the beautiful lines in the poem by the French poet who wrote incandescently about, of all things, soap; and the way light glanced off a bowl of apples in a still life at three o'clock in the afternoon; and what the insightful artist really had in mind when he painted that woman sitting so lonely with her absinthe; and why the man who had loved his piano and the gorgeous, if often haunting music he wrote for it and played on it had finally retreated into utter madness, leaving his desolate and devoted wife behind; and many, many more things.

But she, the small boy's very tall, very all-knowing sister did not, in time, survive; without warning, she departed the earth one afternoon, eaten alive by something inside her that succeeded in devouring her most secret parts. (She departed with her eyes closed; she departed, someone said, seeing something altogether different than what, in those moments, had actually been present before her narrowing eyes.) The small boy, now rather a grown man, has discovered that he is truly astonished that, even so many years after his tall sister's death—more than twenty years, in fact—the event of her being devoured still, in very quiet, very private moments, knocks him utterly to his knees; steals all of his breath; blurs his vision; causes a weary dullness behind his eyes to ache, then really ache; and even impels him (though he rarely does this) to (in the most *un*civilized manner) scream. He is surprised. He remains shocked. Sundered, sometimes. And—and (but then he often cannot summon the proper word). Sundered and surprised that, on particular mornings and afternoons and evenings on the green island of his people's origin and history, he finds himself listening—listening especially when he finds himself beneath heavy star apple trees, touching gently the waists of those dark heavy trees—for the sound of her in the language. For the sound of all of them in the wind-language. In the wind-language of memory and time that, irrespective of his own intentions, returns to him without fail with his own words; words like *I still cannot believe that you are gone*, like *I still hate you so much in so many ways for having gone*. Words like *I cannot stop missing you for being gone, and I will never forget you. Yet sometimes how I wish—yes, sometimes really truly wish—that I could, one day—one night—simply, peacefully, forget you.*

AGAIN, A BOOK OF DREAMS
(REFLECTIONS ON *OUR CARIBBEAN*)

<hr>

In the Introduction to the anthology *Our Caribbean: A Gathering of Lesbian and Gay Writing from the Antilles* (published in 2008), titled "Desire through the Archipelago," I wanted from the outset to manifest how utterly essential to the book's actualization—to say nothing of its initial and subsequent conceptualization—actual desire was. By "desire" I meant, and mean still, a particularly urgent and palpable yearning that, at its core, would doubtless be—indeed, in my circumstance certainly most often was—deeply ineffable. (I consider "ineffable" here in at least two of its meanings: indescribable, but also, taking into account the edginess, illicitness, and "danger" often associated with or projected onto queer people's desires, unspeakable.)

And so in imagining this desire, conjure for a moment if you will the occasionally invoked wanderer in the desert, who in his wisest moments will surely not pray for water; for he will know—or, aiming to keep his psyche intact throughout the stresses of such extreme privation, will need to know—that water's actual appearance would loom before his parched imagination as the cruelest sort of taunt. In wisdom and humility, he will settle instead merely for the sight, just there, off to his left at about one hundred yards or slightly more, of the smallest bit of (but how can it be possible!) green, the smallest leaf of some tenacious weed, from which his cracked lips, in an hour of near-deliverance, might coax some moisture. That moisture, so fleeting, will nonetheless permit him the thought that tonight, at least, he will not die.

I don't in any way mean to overstate the feelings of longing and isolation that, if I'm honest, to such a large degree made—must have helped to make—*Our Caribbean* possible. Recalling the arid landscape that, throughout my youth and into my adult years, seemed filled with Caribbean heterosexually identified writers, and with writers who, irrespective of their rumored or actual same-gender inclinations, invariably publicly identified themselves as individuals interested only in the activities and existences of the opposite gender, underscores in my memory how arid indeed and loudly, even often brutishly heterosexual, that landscape could be, and was. The extant world out of which *Our Caribbean* emerged was, perhaps even more than the serest of deserts, one in which so many heterosexually identified Caribbean writers and scholars simply never acknowledged—and clearly never felt the need to acknowledge, given how marginal many of us and our lives and writings obviously were to them—the fact that many of their literary sistren and brethren were writing from, and about, a very different desire: one that focused on and remained largely centered in the permutations of same-gender interests. The work of many of these writers, and others, stands

tall, on eminently forceful legs, in *Our Caribbean*. It is
work that any sensible person today knows, and would
have known when the work was produced, emerged
against—and often in response to—greatly challenging
odds out of (to say the least) deeply unsupportive land-
scapes; for, the fire-and-damnation rants of the narrow-
minded and ignorant aside, and even putting aside for
a moment the violence that their verbal carnage makes
more possible, can anything be more adverse to a human being's successful growth and development than the
determination to ignore him or her as an actual living
person? The determination to say, *No, you don't exist, and
shouldn't*, in spite of resounding evidence to the contrary?
Or, rather: *You should exist only within this airtight container,
two inches high and three inches wide?*

If even particular dreams were to be kept silent,
how could words possibly speak? If words could not
speak—if they could not speak all of what the speaker
might have wished to say especially in regard to desire,
love, yearning, and again desire—what colossal harm
would such enforced silence ultimately do to the har-
nessed imagination?

Aside from doing someone bodily harm ("bodily
harm" encompassing a wide range of cruelties), or killing them, what can be more psychically injurious than
to make inescapably clear that everything about those
whom the world at large considers *perverse* is simply
wrong: wrong human being, wrong way of being a human (and thus not quite human), wrong way of seeing
and looking, wrong way of thinking, wrong way of liv-

ing, and then of course, very wrong way of loving: for-
midably wrong. But if you just *shut up* and hide it all,
keep well out of sight the disgusting and loathsome and
actually sickening bits, we will, *perhaps*, do our best to ac-
commodate you. To tolerate. We will do our best to pre-
tend that those parts of you don't exist. In the meantime,
please understand that you are most certainly welcome
to die—to die in any number of ways, if the silence we
enforce upon you doesn't itself kill you; and it will ultimately kill you, that silence, as it engenders your social
death . . . the death of your innermost, truest self. The
death of truth, possibility, and the possibility of complete
and fully realized humanity . . . this sort of death also
viewed correctly as annihilation.

Taking into account these considerations and the
multitude of enforced silences that continue to abide today, it is a fact that the writers whose work appears in
Our Caribbean are, in numerous and discrete ways, survivors: people who, in more instances than anyone could
tally, can easily enough narrate their own histories of
censorship, marginalization, ostracism, and—in the instance of witnessing their work's walking (in some cases
sashaying) into the light of day—triumph. I should re-
peat that word, *triumph*; for the realities that it represents
are—again, as any sensible person would understand—in
no way small ones, and were extremely hard-won. By
this measure, I consider the work by all of the anthology's contributors to be both triumphs and triumphant,
in the largest possible sense; as, these several years later, I
recognize the triumph of the book's publication itself: an

historical and tide-changing event made possible by the good, open-handed people at Duke University Press, and especially its wonderful editorial director Ken Wissoker, who recognized that, as we at one point discussed, *Our Caribbean* just could be a book that might help to save lives—save *a* life; the life of someone.

A book that might help something in someone's life, help another person. Help someone fend off silence and annihilation.

To know that *Our Caribbean* helped to save my life is already a great deal: a gift for which gratitude, on my part, is the very least of it.

But then what of all those other people—all those magnificent writers in the collection? Thinking of them and their words, how could one not derive joy from the book? From words? Words are what one lives for, the things that one really breathes. And now, so many words and imaginings from these writers who have served to broaden and deepen Caribbean literary arts and intellectual production well into the future, while contributing to—expanding and once again deepening—discussions in the contexts of gender politics and gender studies, postcolonial studies and theory, African American and Africana studies, black queer studies, black British studies and writing, studies of the subaltern, and more, much more than anyone in these days can possibly imagine. Thus one witnesses in the book a true triumph of words made possible simply by the regarded human imagination—the limitless field which, in this case, provides the largesse of a gathering.

Thomas Glave

When asked on occasion about the title of the anthology's introduction, I have responded by saying that
the "desire" in "Desire through the Archipelago" refers
obviously not only to erotic-romantic yearning, but also
to the very powerful need—mine, at the time—to see
and know that a volume like *Our Caribbean* could actually exist; a need particularly acute since, for most of
my life up until the year of the book's acceptance by
the publisher and its publication two years later, there
had never been any indication that such a volume could
one day really appear. For who would have permitted
such a thing? And wouldn't it be shouted down by all
those who had always tried to make us silent? For perhaps all of my life, I told people—certainly long before
I knew what homosexuality was and what it might possibly "mean" or signify in terms of my own existence—I
had sensed, in the place where shadows precede the sort
of language that precedes direct action, that an entity like
Our Caribbean would not ever be granted actual space in
the world without some sort of exhausting struggle, a
tumult accompanied by sacrifice of some kind; because
even if we, the "other" Caribbean people in question,
had been possible—and of course we had been, since
human life had been present in the region—we had
rarely, as far as I had been able to see, been very visible, at
least not in my little corner of upper St. Andrew, Jamaica.
(Some time later, I learned that this perception had actually been somewhat incorrect, and that in fact I had just
not been looking in the right places, or in as many places
as I might have thought to look. But who knew? Some

others knew at the time, but I didn't.[1]) Absolutely no one during my 1970s childhood in Jamaica ever talked about homosexuals, male or female (or any combination in between), much less about *writing* by *those people.*

Yet somewhere, well beyond that time's imagining and even my own, a book of dreams, folding itself into being in corners of dream-shadows, was becoming *Our Caribbean*; a book that, as I thought some time later (when, as an adult, I could actually envisage it), could never be, yet which somehow, I knew or gradually intuited, had to be. Had to be, for as the years passed, didn't the imagination become more searching, more yearning? Braver, maybe? Didn't it begin to ask questions, say things, such as: *But we must exist. Of course we have to exist.* And even if, at thirteen or sixteen or seventeen years old, I feel that I am the only one here in upper St. Andrew, does that not suggest that there might be an only one over there in Martinique, in Cuba, in Bonaire, in San Andrés, in Antigua, in Haiti, in Puerto Rico? What is that only one saying, doing, thinking? What does that only one dream about and desire? Who is that only one?

I began to learn that, in Jamaica at any rate, there were many more of "us" during the time that I began to become a "man." But I also recall an afternoon just before that cardinal time, during which, as the teenager whose life I ended up surviving, I actually did put my hands on several young Jamaican men my own age—put my hands on them and received theirs on me until, on particular afternoons, I and another young man, both of us for some reason dressed in cricket whites and both of us approximately sixteen years old, found some impossibly secret place in a relative's house, his or mine, where we hid ourselves away, and there and there again pressed against each other—pressed to summon and feel the warmth, the charge, and the unmistakable pulsing of the jet-black bird in the smooth white center of the orchid's throat. *Not the only one.* Desire. The years.

And so as articulating language gradually became more possible, so loomed another word toward the shaping of the book of dreams: conversation. What was the conversation that surely must have been taking place between Caribbean writers writing "queer"-ness, moving through the erotics of same-gender attractions? Between writers in the Caribbean conjuring, inventing and reinventing and imagining and reimagining "queer"-ness, and those engaged in similar activities in the Caribbean's far-reaching diaspora? Between Caribbean people of same-gender erotic inclination and the rest of the world? Between those solidly situated in "empire," invested in it, and those who refused to acknowledge their relationship to "empire"? Between those who, correctly or not, saw themselves as part of the British Caribbean, others as part of the French or Dutch, and those who saw themselves as unquestionably—or questionably—part of Latin America?

And what about those who saw themselves as part of the region known as "Latin America *and* the Caribbean"? In fact the profound connections between the two began to make more immediate sense to me after traveling in the early 1990s as a student to Guatemala, Colombia,

Peru, Ecuador, and other countries in South America, and then a few years later to the Dominican Republic and Cuba, and seeing, hearing, and smelling for myself the similarities between all of them and "the Caribbean"; and then again after the good fortune of journeying through Galeano's *Las venas abiertas de América latina,* as well as García Márquez's *One Hundred Years of Solitude* and *Chronicle of a Death Foretold*: after such journeys and some thinking and observation and remembering, realizing, of course: absolutely. We are each other's people. Each other's blood.

Blood like that produced by a machete's dangerous swing, when a young poor Trinidadian woman named Elizete, unexpectedly distracted from drudgery by her own desire for another woman as they both labored beneath a fierce sun in a cane field in which they both might have labored fifty or one hundred or two hundred years before, sliced open her own foot while mesmerized by "[t]hat woman like a drink of cool water. The four o'clock light thinning she dress": so remarked Elizete, rapt with desire, in Dionne Brand's "Elizete, Beckoned," excerpted in *Our Caribbean* from Brand's lyrical novel *In Another Place, Not Here.* In that other unmistakably Caribbean place, a cane field that after hundreds of years could not stop whispering *slavery, this earth, colonialism, right here,* Brand showed us vulnerable women desiring each other's flesh and mouths in Trinidad, and daring— as Elizete dared—to turn away from the men who forced them into unwanted sexual couplings simply because, as always, those men could. Elizete: poor, uneducated, black, and trapped for some time (but not forever) in that cane field, at one point trapped also beneath the body of Isaiah, the black man who "owned" her: laying beneath him mute, unresponsive, and resistant in her muteness, she dreamt only of that other woman, whose arms, glance, kisses, and very breath would transport her to another place: one of liberation, fulfillment, and the body and depth of another woman, not there.

Through the centuries and up to now, there were many others like Elizete: in another place still, the poor and working-class women in Suriname who, during their daily work upon the lands they mostly didn't own and had little chance of owning, sang love songs to each other in the twentieth century, as they had done in earlier centuries, as the Surinamese scholar Gloria Wekker's historical-ethnographic work on "mati" women, also included in *Our Caribbean*, observed. There were the many unspeaking, and, recalling Morrison's phrase from *Beloved, disremembered and unaccounted for* women who desired other women, such as those described in the Jamaican writer Makeda Silvera's cornerstone essay "Man Royals and Sodomites: Some Thoughts on the Invisibility of Afro-Caribbean Lesbians," in which, moving through and toward a kind of recovery project of silenced and disremembered Jamaican women's voices—the voices of mostly rural-situated women who, as Silvera discovered, loved, desired, and sometimes had erotic-romantic relationships with other women—the author wrested from disremembrance women like Miss Poinsettia, known by those in the small town in which she lived as someone who was "so" or "that way," but not necessarily scorned. Silvera's writing disclosed a little of the life of someone like Miss Jonesie, cut off from the love she seemed so much to need, and an ultimate prisoner of the alcohol without which she eventually could not live. Explorations and recoveries like Silvera's disclose not only the wide geography of dreams that encompass and embody both life and literature; such explorations also reveal the possibilities of a literature *for* life, that breathes and is life: the kind of literature that enables survival because it says (or shouts), *But wait, because I am here, and I exist.* The kind of literature that works vigorously against the constant silence that destroys both soul and body and limits the imagination of both the definer and the defined.

Where had all these invisible people been throughout history? The men who had yearned for other men; the women who had sought (or not sought, not dared to seek) other women. Where had they been on the plantations?—for, as Brand illustrated, they had most definitely been there, as both owned and owner—and overseer. Whipped or carved, disemboweled or hanged, burned or muzzled, sold or traded or maimed or raped and raped and raped, they had been there. Had been on the ships that brought so many people to the region in devastatingly unthinkable numbers . . . ever more bodies of the disremembered and unaccounted for . . . so that, in keeping with the general fate of the disremembered, some will forever be truly lost and forgotten, unknown, because so very few people have ever been interested in looking for them.

Thomas Glave

But now, more than ever, I hope, we can re-member more of them: put them back together, and ourselves, as, putting best feet forward, we proceed. Proceed along the road of humanity, farther away from disremembrance and loathing. Farther from hatred.

Not long ago, I told someone something that I have shared more than once with a few friends: that one of the reasons I loved and continue to love the great choreographer George Balanchine ("Mr. B." to those who knew, loved, learned from, and danced for him), several of whose ballets I learned when a dance student and later when I was an actual grown-up dancer, was (is) because of his quietly disciplined work ethic and his simple, clear-as-water ease of expression. When asked once by an interviewing journalist how he managed to choreograph so many ballets over the course of his long and prolific career—ballets that were so consistently beautiful and brilliant—he calmly, matter-of-factly responded, "Well, dear, you see, the people come, and they pay, so I have to make a ballet for them." I would like to think that many of the life principles that I learned in ballet have remained at the center of my consciousness in my postballet life, an awareness of the necessity for discipline among them; and so perhaps a Balanchinean pragmatism arose and subliminally (or consciously) guided me when, one day early in this century, I realized that *Our Caribbean* was a book that didn't exist, that had never existed—and so I would have to make it. Make it so that the people could come and read it, as I too would be able to do upon its completion.

And so, after five and a half years of work, there, one afternoon, we were: thirty-seven writers from fourteen different countries in the veritable shape of what struck me, suddenly, as a kind of community, although—at least as far as I could see—an untested one, largely uncharted, and constantly—if only due partly to literal and literary movements between "home" and diaspora—in flux. For me, these realities could at least suggest that *Our Caribbean* might in actuality move toward (and assist one, in thinking and reflection, to move more toward) both the idea *and reality* of *our* Caribbean: that is, the place(s) that may or may not have been "home" but that nonetheless, as much as we wish them to be, are *ours*; what might at long last "belong" to "us," as much as a region can belong to anyone—belong to those of us who are "that way" and who consider ourselves Antillean, whomever we may be and however we may or may not ultimately identify ourselves. Those Caribbeans, as reimagined and reconfigured spaces and actual places, might be, to play slightly with Dionne Brand's poetic title, our very places, right there.

Taking these considerations slightly further, the "our" of *Our Caribbean* also suggests to me that ideas of and about "the Caribbean," and representations of it, can also be ours—that is, that the particular sensibilities that we as same-gender-inclined people develop in response to the world and our discrete worlds at large can also play a part in the Caribbean's imaginative, intellectual, and artistic growth (and in this process we have anyway of course already had a long-standing part, even if and when we were not readily visible or identifiable, including the many times people did not wish to identify us as same-gender-inclined). The words in the book's title remind me that those of us who make it our task to do so can now more than ever challenge that which has invariably worked most effectively in our silent self-censoring: shame and the power of shame.

But finally the words of the volume's title additionally suggest, for me, the Caribbeans that we as same-gender-interested people continually create and reshape entirely for ourselves; sometimes in plain sight of heterosexually identified people, and sometimes far beyond any social reality or space they have ever known, given homophobia's segregating power and the frequent unwillingness (or inability) of many heterosexually identified people to acknowledge queerness around them in daily life: the public and private spaces that we make "queer" or *more* "queer." (I think of carnival, for example, but also remember the profoundly homosocial and homoerotic energy of cricket matches, and the powerful lesbierotic energy present in some female-centered and -administered households.) Indeed, our very presence—at least when that presence is acknowledged as "queer"— radically challenges gender-binary thinking and rigid thinking about gender roles, as our queerness "troubles" both questions and notions about absolute categories of sexuality, gender, and race. In these regards, one might closely consider Caribbean, and other, interracial same-gender sexual and romantic couplings; or, for one's own imaginative and intellectual amplification, imagine which woman in the market might secretly be kissing which other woman, which man in the cane field or the rumshop might later find himself atop or beneath which other man, and look over there at the calypso band: is that woman a man or a woman, or a man-woman beating pon de drums, and is she-he-she black or brown or white or yellow or something? And if a man of one color is squeezing, with his very large hands, the batty or the bam-bam of another; if a woman who looks as if she could be this race or that one, or from this social class or that one, is publicly, without fear or shame, moving her face over the breasts of another woman, do we care? And then, caring or not, what are the ways in which we challenge time-honored perceptions about "the nation" and especially the (often unacknowledged, except by some feminist scholars, and sometimes not even by them) patriarchal nation; and more.

And so maybe through one million permutations can sail the life—the lives—of a book of dreams: one that, with great fortune, might one of these nights or days transform even to a book of complete light, if it hasn't already done so. A book bearing both light and darkness within its leaves. A book of dreams and shifting light, a book of desire, that might do something toward honoring the memory of the uncountable disremembered and unaccounted for . . . even only a small breath. A libation of quiet words. Just something like *At last. Finally.* For you.

JAMAICAN, OCTOPUS

The unity is submarine.
—Kamau Brathwaite, *Contradictory Omens*

Octopus? But yes. The idea, or rather reality, of my-self as an octopus—and as what I actually now know myself to be, *Hapalochlaena lunulata*, the greater blue-ringed octopus, as opposed to what I would really often prefer to be, *Octopus vulgaris*, the common octopus—emerged earlier this year as a more or less private joke with a friend; a joke with (as that friend understood it) a distinctly erotic center well-rooted in manifestations of a sort of intimate "queerness," if you will, between us: a queerness experienced not so much as frank desire but rather as intimate and tacit understanding between us of our discrete and generally verbally unexpressed, most se-cret desires: an understanding that this friend articulated between us only in the lowest and most private of tones. It was in this time with him that I was able, unlike him, to slip more comfortably into my other skin, or skins, flesh and fleshes, of octopus, order of *Octopoda*, a simple but complex well-evolved and evolving mollusk.

I proceed into this writing with the awareness that I'm trying very hard—and the task is difficult—to work,

move, even swim, sentence by sentence, toward a language that might in some way capture, represent, even
directly (or at least figuratively) illustrate, the ways and
hows of becoming the varying and occasionally connected whos whom I wish (and sometimes, depending
on the day and environment, do not wish) to be: writer/
artist, political activist, "intellectual."[1]

And so, toward exploration of a kind—my own non-
linear journey into a sort of interior—I must consider
octopuses. Queer creatures. And mutable. Mutable in
form, to a degree, and size, although not, unlike some
other sea creatures, mutable in gender; creatures that possess the ability to change shape (and thus avoid detection) and color (and so also avoid detection), and that
regularly seek invisibility and camouflage, invisibility by
way of camouflage. Creatures both predatory and preyed
upon, life-threatened by innumerable enemies and even
by their own mating exercises and cycles of pregnancy,
they seek to remain unseen, or at least largely often un-
recognizable as octopuses. (Consider, for example, the
Amphioctopus marginatus: the octopus that, rather than
jetting away from danger in a cloud of dark ink that dis-
orients predators and slightly disables an enemy's sense
of smell, actually ambles away on two feet, or "arms,"
looking very much like a moving or even swaying plant.
Incidentally, octopus ink is partly composed of melanin,
which also inhabits my skin and the skin of all humans,
and is found in innumerable other species. Another link
between all of us and this mutable cephalopod.)

And then remember—I certainly must remember—

that all octopuses can, if the danger is dire enough and chance of escape seems slim, detach one or more of their limbs, by way of autotomy: a danger-evasion tactic exercised also by some reptiles, spiders, and lobsters. *Autotomy*, from the Late Greek, meaning essentially a severing or amputation of the self. Such severing obviously differs from the life-enabling process of *evisceration*, through which some invertebrate sea creatures may, when facing grave conditions, expel their own internal organs, and later regenerate them.

I think of the dear octopus as a sort of queer subject: a creature possessed of not only two, but eight arms, in an environment in which fins, far more than arms, are common (although octopuses do also have gills); and a creature generally possessed of three hearts, as if one somehow were not enough, and not enough trouble, all told. Octopus, that is not at all a fish, really nothing like one, in an environment populated mainly—at least on the face of it—by fishes; an environment in which nothing else quite like the octopus exists, not even its traveling cousin the squid. A world in which one often must change color or shape in order to evade detection by enemies, and death. As someone who writes, I, unlike the octopus, am neither predatory (as far as I know) nor preyed upon (as far as I know), yet I invariably seek to be unseen. By "seek to be unseen," I mean that in the realm through which many writers—perhaps especially writers of fiction and poetry—at some point or another swim, the blue realm of (hopefully) fathomless imagining, one seeks to disappear, to remove one's *I*-ness from the landscape; from those subaqueous depths where the most uninhibited imagining begins, can begin, even though it is in that place above all others where I, still casting aside my I-ness, remain among the octopuses and more easily become one of them. One of them, those queer subjects and creatures, since it is through imagining and actual feeling, and even (especially) dreaming, that I follow them and then follow and become the principal thing itself; that is, even beyond the watchful octopuses (knowing as they do that danger always lurks just beyond today's cave), I become the voice in the story, the people or octopuses in the story: the story not yet written, that must be written. The story that is being written down there in the blue place of dreams and imagining where queer creatures hide and leave their arms behind for sharks (dumbfounded at the prey's brisk and unexpected escape) to swallow. As the writer, I am not "I": in this ideal world, the world of blue and shadow and octopuses and even sharks—and certainly, if unfortunately, crabs—I become nothing and nobody, as the voices and the people, and the cephalopods, emerge.

And they do emerge. But then what has any of this to do with Jamaica, with the Caribbean, or at least with my Caribbean? What has any of this discussion of octopuses and their ink (and I haven't even begun to say anything about their startling intelligence and playfulness, nor about their problem-solving skills and ability to work with tools) have to do with the Caribbean that I know?

At this point I should make clear that the first time

I drowned—the first of at least four such incidents, in fact—was in Jamaica; in eastern Jamaica, to be precise, when I was a child. I was about twelve years old at the time, and constantly curious about everything: about the sea, certainly, and the (still, to this day) dearly cherished south coast, with its dark heavy sand and thick knottings of palms along the shores. I was curious about the stars of all time, in which, on nights preceding storms, I had often envisaged the sad and sometimes elongated faces of African saints, that astral light still veiling their most elusive desires; and of course I remained powerfully curious about the quite elderly man who, as I knew at the time, had one day rather unremarkably crawled up out of the sea on his long octopus-colored legs. (And so imagine if you will in his skin the shifting tones of primordial sand, light to dark to light.)

It was at this juncture—around the time that I drowned for the first time, when I met the elderly octopus-colored gentleman—that my true, undeniable journey into a kind of queerness began. While this journey did begin in Jamaica, I would be more accurate if I told you that it began more literally in the Caribbean Sea, in the sea of my ancestors . . . in what I have always known, personally and primordially, as the Sea of We. Began there as, on that salmon-toned early morning, the elderly octopus-colored gentleman, his skin smooth as a young eel's, pulled me into the sea with him: pulled me as if I were a recalcitrant pup on a leash (although I had not yet, at that time, glimpsed or made special note of leashes on animals or humans in Jamaica); pulled me along without a struggle into the waves, the waters, into the blue and green depths of what would become my deeper venturing into—into—

Was the—*is* the—"_____" at the end of that preceding sentence unspeakable? Unwriteable? Whether it was or not, whether it is today or not, an empty space remains there. Those who know may claim that an octopus will soon curl sucking arms about it, as the foam of the sea washes over and caresses it in this present-day time as—so we know now from our difficult history—also occurred in earlier times.

And in some ways I do blame him, that elderly gentleman. Blame him for the later inconveniences and disruptions that I suffered and continue to suffer in life. For it was he after all who, so steadfastly pulling me into the waves that day, caused me to drown for the first time; and it was only after I emerged again from the sea some hours later that I realized that, with this brief sojourn into the depths of octopuses and rays, cuttlefish and blueheads, my life had forever altered. Years later, men in whose glances my dreams and wondering fingers expressed a sustained interest would express irritation, if not outright outrage, at my constant need, even during intimate moments, to momentarily remove myself from their overtures or embraces, and dash to a sink or bathtub—invariably theirs—in order to fill it rapidly with water (warm water, of course), so that I might immerse myself completely in it (*a blessing*, I would think, *but also often a trial, an unexpected urgency*), and breathe it as if drowning (but so gently, calmly, inevitably, unfearfully): breathe it, drink it, smell it, conjure it, remember it, and (though to them it was nothing more than water running from a tap) taste in it the salt water of my earliest memories and of so many suction-cupped arms that, in another life, had without fail caressed and protected me: the arms of a queer creature that, like some of the ghosts I had long known—duppies, demons, and the occasionally irritating, sometimes interfering, always watchful presences of those in my infinite familial line who had walked the earth hundreds and even thousands of years before—could change color and shape. My face would remain beneath those sink or bathtub waters for minutes, sometimes for as long as a half hour's time, as I breathed and drowned once again and ultimately, to my lover's disbelief or terror, emptied the vessel of all liquid. And what a thing it would be, then, to swallow completely water poured into a tub in which (as you discerned more plainly upon your immersion) your lover's body had previously left a gritty ring he hadn't successfully cleaned away, or simply hadn't bothered to clean away. How much more quickly the blood beat then, your blood, as, upon observing that he had just completed one of his rare baths (for like so many modern individuals he usually preferred showering), you lowered your face into that water in which on that particular evening he had perhaps lightly (or forcefully, with much salt) urinated, or, with luck, more than one time, broken his typically cataclysmic wind. What a thing to drown yourself again in his sink, conjuring cephalopods rubbing, rubbing against your skin, as you felt yourself harden, harden more against the sink countertop, as, with

eyes completely closed, you raised your dripping face
out of the sink water . . . and dear God, how good and
indeed necessary it felt to drown again that time, even
though by then you had most likely frightened off that
lover also, frightened him away for all time: for recall
how, after drowning yourself in his waters, he regarded
you with such open-eyed terror; indeed, with such horror, as if you were a creature from the beyond (which
in fact you were and are). And so of course he couldn't
possibly comprehend, as none of them ever could or will,
the enormity of what the elderly gentleman showed you
that day beneath the sea: what you learned while down
there, and, most important, by way of repeated drown-
ings in lovers' sinks, bathtubs, and other vessels, what has
been retained.

If I were completely dead instead of as fully, implaca-
bly alive as I am right now, I would tell everyone, including my most secret and unknowable best beloved, exactly
what I learned and saw beneath the sea that day, in the
guiding grasp of the elderly octopus-colored gentleman,
back deh so inna Jamaica, right deh so. I would tell everyone how at last, down there, as I drowned and drowned
again, I could see that we were free, at last free, I mean
really *free*. I could see as the young boy I was that, in the
Sea of We, the "we" was, in part, a group of men assem-
bled at the place to which the elderly gentleman, under
the sea, directly took me; at least they looked somewhat
like "men," although one remembers that it isn't always
easy beneath the sea to know for certain what exactly
men should look like. They were completely undressed,

utterly and even (strikingly) defenselessly naked. They seemed jubilant, they seemed exhilarated, they appeared to be of all ages, and some of them had drowned repeatedly over a lifetime, or more than one, whereas others, like me, were drowning for only the first time. I believe that some of them had hair and flesh the color of the waves by then so far above us, although of course I can't ever be entirely sure—so many memories, *except* for the smell, touch, strong grip, and muscular suck of octopus, fade over the years. And so it was the elderly gentleman himself who told me that they were in such a state of jubilation, those more-or-less men, because, "Here, under the sea," the gentleman told me, gazing calmly into my eyes through the dappled waters (and even at depths of thirty feet and more, he never released my hand from what I now understand was a protective grip; for indeed, if anything tragic or untoward had happened to me, who would have answered to my parents and family, but him?)—"Here, under the sea," he continued, turning to gaze off at the cavorting men (I remain amazed to this day by their phenomenal flexibility: for by this time they had each begun to execute perfect somersaults that vaulted effortlessly only inches above stands of fearsomely dagger-sharp coral[2])—

"Here," he went on, "they are happy, we are happy, because everyone, each one of us, has—"

But he did not have to finish that momentous sentence: I knew what he was going to say. Each of the more-or-less men had a—had an actual pussy: a male pussy, some would say; a (depending on your geographi-

cal origin) manpussy or man's pussy, or whatever else
so many above the waves might choose to call it. My
twelve-year-old eyes saw and instantly understood: *Pussy,*
I thought, *yes, exactly. A site, for some, of pleasure.* (Don't
ask me how, at twelve years old, growing up in a strictly
conservative and even parochial Anglican middle-class
Jamaican family, I knew such a thing with certainty, or
even how I knew a phrase such as "site of pleasure"—
but I did, I assure you, as surely as pigs grunt and dogs
sniff.) *Site of pleasure,* I thought, stunned, and even jubilant. For if *they*, cavorting and somersaulting, leaping
and balancing, could have a pussy, then I knew I could as
well. I would remember over the years that this sort of
pussy would not necessarily have anything to do with—
be required to have anything to do with—the ways in
which the more-or-less men had removed each other's
penises during the somersault frolicking, and the dark
open space that remained long after the penis had been
removed. This pussy could instead reside out of sight
between their tightly clenched buttocks, where most of
them continued to grip those still erect penises; and for
all anyone knows, it might reside elsewhere still.

But then who, given contemporary headlines and
news reports of guaranteed local mayhem and rage,
would ever have imagined that such revelry could have
existed in Jamaica, in a place some thirty or forty feet
beneath the sea, along the terrain where earthquakes
had snuffled and bellowed in past centuries? Who, given
so much of what we have heard about Jamaica's fury
in recent decades, would ever have imagined that not

only octopuses could dart and jet and jettison their arms among the corals, but that more-or-less men, sometimes drowned and sometimes not, could delight in the actuality of their pussies even as they exulted and somersaulted with a brethren's automatized penis in their celebrating hands? Who could have imagined that the only colors that would be of any consequence down there would be the color, oh, the *colors*, of octopus, *Octopus*!—Octopus Sheen, Octopus Brillante, Octopus Gleam—along my elderly gentleman's forearms and lean, smooth, long legs, and the colors of sea and sky and sun and stars and moon and light and dark and gray and green and blue and yellow and living and dead and breath and sound (or soundlessness, the color of utter soundlessness, hearable at the bottom of the sea more, much more, than anywhere else on earth)—those colors alone that would dapple and stipple over the skins of those (surely, if I remember correctly) also octopus-colored more-or-less men? *And so color me in thy tones, Sea,* I thought or prayed immediately upon the heels of this first as it were initiatory drowning, *so that Yea, I may yet be free. Free,* I thought, or prayed. Who would ever have known? For the sea revealed nothing of these unknowns to any of us—to any of us living in Jamaica at the time—and the moon, indifferent as always to events beyond its control, did not, either.

I remain convinced to this day that it was above all because of this youthful experience so far beneath the waves, in a place where I had mostly felt safe and often happy (my beloved south shore of the island, not far from the agreeable beach in the parish of St. Thomas to which my family always drove, on a Sunday, for swimming and relaxation)—happy in a place where, in the company of my conservative Anglican family, though I never directly saw again those more-or-less men nor the elderly gentleman who had befriended me and helped me to drown and return, I knew that they all were there, somewhere—I remain convinced to this day that it was because of this experience that I was able to write, many years later, a work of fiction that, set in contemporary Jamaica, centers in part on a middle-class "brown," "respectable" man who, though he yearns so much for a (darker, poorer) fisherman to penetrate him in his "pussy," knows that, as the married, respectable, middle-class, evidently lucid male that he is, he dare not ever speak aloud of his "pussy."[3] He seems to know that only in his innermost places may he freely, unabashedly beg the (darker, poorer) object of his desire to "breed" him and "fuck him inna" his "pussy." He appears to know, as innumerable men in so many places seem to believe, that he dare not ever, not *ever*, speak aloud such words: unutterable words, unthinkable, even by many men who frankly desire other men. The character in the fiction seems to feel what many men, at different times, have felt: that the word "pussy" conjures for many of them the most hated and feared thing of all—a womanish thing, as in a womanish man: a man who has a "pussy" instead of a _____ (please fill in the blank); a man who does not necessarily put above all else his cock, and opts instead, as many men do, to be plunged: to be bored through well into the depths of his previously unknown and unknowable, unspeakable pussy. And so perhaps it can indeed be possible for a writer of fiction who has tried his very best to live *and survive* in octopus skin—survive if only for a few minutes, even—to write, and imagine, such unthinkable, unspeakable words. Unspeakable words and realities that I first witnessed beneath the sea, but also heard presented directly to me over the years, in Jamaica and elsewhere, out of the mouths of more-or-less men, in phrases (usually whispered, but sometimes shouted in the most guaranteed-private spaces) such as *Put it deep-deep inna mi pussy*, or, *Jesus Christ have mercy, gwan and kiss mi pussy, nuh, man?* or, *Oh God, God, what a way you hood feel good*, good, *man!—inna mi pussy*. And then of course at all the parties and gatherings in Jamaica where men kissed and touched and held one another, greeted one another with kisses and even on occasion with sound slaps across the forgiving and often welcoming backside (although it could also be quite resistant), one had heard those words as well: at all the parties where de bwoy dem would kick up dem frock and go on like Miss Mattie or Miss Whomever, one had heard some of the more fear-less ones, the more brazen and inveterate and reckless ones, talk about their pussy. I had not been dreaming. I dreamt often beneath the sea, but rarely on land, at least not until I departed Jamaica.

After all these years, whether or not I myself ever made remarks such as those I had heard, I remain grateful to the more-or-less men who, so freely, performed those acrobatics beneath the waves, and so gently, yet firmly, assuredly, detached each other's penises for the onward journey that ultimately became those penises' destiny. It is really because of those more-or-less men, and the elderly gentleman who so guided me, that I have been able to write these ostensibly unspeakable things in books, in stories; for, as anyone who knows me knows, I do not, and will not ever, write anything in a book that is not grounded in and proven by hard, incontrovertible fact: the sort of concrete "truths" without which the West, for example, cannot long survive, or at least continue envisioning itself as "the West." The sort of incontrovertible facts and "truths" which have no doubt contributed to our existences today. The sort of facts that make octopuses and melanin-filled ink possible; that make evisceration, automatization, and public beheadings possible; that make possible a man desperate to consume the closest water within reach finally unconcerned about drinking all of the water out of his lover's dirt-ringed bathtub or unwashed kitchen sink; that man drowning as he drinks, knowing all the while that his drinking is as possible, and sometimes as necessary, as drowning. For I will say again now what I have already said several times: that I and others like me have drowned many times. We have drowned innumerable times and have returned with the sea and so much more in our lungs and in all our secret, not yet eviscerated or automatized places; returned to the places and times in which, in spite of our drowning and certain need to drown in the future, so much, for each of us in so many different ways, still remains possible.

And what have I learned, do I continue to learn, from my beloved octopus, as even now, ever mischievous (though it is about time for this mischief to *stop*), it hides from me particular strategies for survival, or merely for living? *But everything*, the sea murmurs back to me, inviting me even now to walk into it without the guidance of my elderly gentleman; inviting me, that golden-skinned sea, to descend once again into it in order to (as if I were a trained seal) complete a few somersaults, and finish by holding in my by then completely wrinkled hands a penis. Perhaps a shark's this time, or the time-toughened penis-cock of an older woman, heavy hoary balls and all. *Everything*, those waters murmur to me once more; and at this point, sluggishly aware of the somnolence that the sea's air always casts upon me, it is easy enough to simply summon once again the smell of octopus—that smell, unlike any other—as I feel its arms wrapping once again about me and that flesh, octopus sucker-flesh, moving all over me, over every part of my flesh, once again. Easy enough to heed the sea now, heed it, as, way out there, upon it, in it, soon to be once again beneath it, I move slightly, then cease all movement. As I look up at the sky once more, but *only* once; then finally close my eyes gently. Close them, then throw back my head. Throw it back, just like this, as if maybe drowning, in order to feel, and breathe, and *breathe*, and listen.

FIVE WRITERS,
NO PRECIOUSNESS,
AND A NOT-POEM

Andrew Salkey's *Escape to an Autumn Pavement*: An Introduction

A
among the twentieth century's Caribbean-born
writers who at one time or another emigrated
to Britain—C.L.R. James, Samuel Selvon, Beryl Gilroy, Wilson Harris, George Padmore, Claudia Jones, and
George Lamming among them—Andrew Salkey, born
in Panama to Jamaican parents in 1928, remains one of
the most arresting and original. While numerous Caribbean writers of the period expressed their anger about
and opposition to British colonialism in the West Indies,
British racism, and the often traumatizing plights of Caribbean emigrants in England—as their descendants did
later in the century and continue to do today—none attempted as bold a journey into explorations of sexuality,
and the possible homosexuality of a Caribbean man in
particular, as did Salkey in his novel *Escape to an Autumn
Pavement*.[1]

In *Escape*, accompanying Salkey through his crisp,
often terse prose, we encounter a London all at once
familiar, public, yet revealed as a terrain of secrets: a landscape of vulnerabilities as emotionally charged as they
are profoundly and (for a little while, at least) unspeak-
ably private. This is the city of Hampstead Heath and
Piccadilly, but also of ardently experienced, sometimes

ambivalently propelled desire felt by one man for another, and by a woman and man for each other—the sorts of complicated interracial and intercultural desires that here anticipate the more overt sexual experimentation to come later in the decade. It is through these complex and compelling attractions that we soon come to know Johnnie Sobert, the novel's sardonically articulate, deeply conflicted Jamaican protagonist who, by his own description, is "middle class. Or so I've been made to think."

Escape to an Autumn Pavement places us squarely in the London of 1960–61, fifteen years after the end of World War II and nineteen years after the German blitzkrieg of London and several other cities in Britain that took more than forty thousand lives in the capital alone, and whose results were still visible in vacant bombsites. Britain still maintains colonies in the Caribbean, Africa, and Asia, though with increasing dissent and resistance from the colonized. Johnnie Sobert's London is the increasingly racially uneasy, twilight-empire city that, twelve years after the arrival there of the famous *Empire Windrush* ship with emigrants mostly from Jamaica and other parts of the Anglophone Caribbean, reveals an increasingly African-descended—and specifically Antillean—population. It is a metropole that continues to house the royal family and parliament, but also many West Indian nightclubs, such as the one in which Johnnie works in Oxford Circus, squarely in the heart of the face-shifting city. In 1962, only a year after we meet Johnnie, Jamaica, accompanied by Trinidad and followed four years later by Barbados, will become an independent nation no longer formally beholden to "Mother" England.

In *Escape*, we share the observations of a shrewd Caribbean man's eye—an eye deeply skeptical of Britain and its pretensions and hypocrisies—in Johnnie's typically witheringly ironic comments on English citizens and life:

> Astringent faces in the queue; behind me clock-faces, all with tea-time written over them—tea-time past and tea-time to come. What a good shot of Jamaican white rum wouldn't do for them is nobody's business! Come on, now, we must learn to love our neighbours as ourselves. Learn to be tolerant (good word that! A damn' good British-made word!)

As *Escape* progresses, Johnnie's acerbic observations about English and Caribbean people and society loom as the insights of someone powerfully unsettled not only sexually, as his continual self-questioning and pondering of possible attraction to another man—a white Englishman—increases, but also geographically and psychically. He is an urban London outsider far from the Caribbean "home" about which he has a profound ambivalence, yet to which he still feels in some ways a deep emotional connection, as he makes clear in a passionate critique of Jamaica's class difficulties in a revealing conversation with Fiona Trado, a white Englishwoman who discloses to Johnnie that she has a romantic-sexual "past" with a

Nigerian, and is presently—restively—wife of the man who collects rents for the rooming house where Johnnie lives. Johnnie tells us:

There's no middle-class bit where I come from. Yet there's a sort of behaviour which adds up to it. Which damn' well strangles everybody. The thing doesn't exist, yet a tight bunch of people move and hope and act as if they're being guided by it . . . Surely it takes much more than a hundred and twenty-eight years after the Abolition of Slavery for a middle class to evolve?

Later in the novel, in a sequence of reflections on his difficult relationship with his father ("the old man"), Johnnie's perspectives on the Jamaican middle class and the implicit reasons for his "escape" from that context become even more trenchant:

I suppose [the old man] had the right life saved up for me. The life of endless respectable pursuits and conventional patterns of behaviour. Not that the old man would have insisted. But "the others" would have prescribed a girl three to four shades lighter than myself. Respectable people are married people. Shade's the thing. Could very well be the reason for my coming to England where I can get a girl a million shades lighter than myself. Just to show the Jamaican and Panamanian middle-classery where it gets off.

This anger and restlessness, manifested in Johnnie's unyielding desire to question and critique the painful realities left behind at "home" and the newer, more immediate inconsistencies and peculiarities everywhere about him (including the erotic and platonic possibilities that arise in the Oxford Circus nightclub where he works as a waiter, and the interactions between other West Indians whom he meets there), marks the sharpening of a Jamaican consciousness in conflict with the emergence of a Caribbean-British hybrid one; a way of being that today could be correctly termed black British: an identity comfortable with both blackness and "British"-ness, derived from the deeply complex perspectives of both, that squares with the fact that blackness and Britishness are not mutually exclusive. In Johnnie, the result of these convergences and tensions is a kind of insider-outsider eye that, throughout the novel, wields a wicked ability to skewer characters and situations. Among the most hilarious and disturbing of these skewerings is a moment with a drunk white Englishman who casually chats Johnnie up outside a pub early one evening, starting with what can only be described as a decidedly odd conversation opening, the strangely intimate imperiousness of which reflects the colonial relationship between them ("Where d'you come from, young man? . . . Come on, answer smartly, now. I won't bite you, you know"). After learning that Johnnie is Jamaican, the Englishman tactlessly remarks, "You've got some very beautiful women, haven't you? Wonderful skin. Nice high backsides. Strong devils,

I bet?" In a subsequent moment both shocking but also grotesquely comic and revealing, this man frankly confides that he would like to "get my hands on one of those nigger wenches. Delightful people!"

It is also fascinating to note *Escape*'s anticipation of, and conversation with, the conflicts expressed in Derek Walcott's famous poem "A Far Cry from Africa," published in 1962, a full two years after *Escape*. Walcott's poem centers on the anxieties raised in a "fractured" consciousness (similar to W.E.B. Du Bois's African American "double consciousness" theory, espoused nearly sixty years earlier) that, from minute to minute, migrates uneasily between the "West" and an historically remembered and embraced Africa. In this tense exchange with Fiona, Johnnie notes:

". . . I walk around London and I see statues of this one and the other . . . I see litters of paintings in your museums and galleries. St Paul's. The Tower. All of them. There's even Stonehenge! And d'you know how I feel deep down? . . . I feel nothing at all! And yet, I want to feel just a little something."

"But why?"

"Why? Because Africa doesn't belong to me! There's no feeling there. No bond. We've been fed on the Mother Country myth. Its language. Its history. Its literature . . . We feel chunks of it rubbing off on us. We believe in it. We trust it. Openly, we admit we're a part of it. But are we? Where's the real link?"

Walcott's ideologically and personally risky poem, full of profound and brilliantly deployed prismatic ironies and searing, unanswerable questions for the writer and human being, such as "...how choose/Between this Africa and the English tongue I love?" and "How can I turn from Africa and live?" garnered considerable attention after its publication.[2]

Keeping in mind Salkey's formidable skill with precisely honed language—language that, sometimes playful, sometimes grave, and often ambiguous in regard to sexual and romantic desire, frequently veils as much as it discloses, opting more for implication over direct statement—it is Johnnie's attraction to another man, and what is gradually revealed about that man's feelings toward him, that comprise some of the most fascinating moments in *Escape*. All of this is bravely rendered by Salkey in an era when the word "homosexuality," to say nothing of the homosexuality of a Caribbean person, was not only unmentionable, but literally unthinkable. An interracial relationship between two men that involved actual love and romance was surely even more beyond the pale, as, in many instances, remains the case today.

Reading *Escape to an Autumn Pavement* again, as Peepal Tree Press has fortunately made it possible to do with its reissued edition of the novel in the beautifully produced Caribbean Modern Classics series, I remain grateful to both the author and the press for making Johnnie Sobert's story available to an entirely new generation of readers, among them Caribbean readers, Caribbean queer readers, queer readers everywhere, and innumerable others. It is not unrealistic to imagine that Salkey, who died in 1995, would not only have been pleased with the gorgeous new edition of his novel; I believe he would have applauded, and perhaps, as Johnnie would have been inclined to do, even laughed, sardonically yet with appreciation, out loud; then invited us all to Johnnie's Oxford Circus West Indian club for a round of good Jamaican white rum, glasses raised to resounding and emphatic cheers.

Finsbury Park, London
January 2009

The Four of Them

Gordimer

But then during a particular time, in that beleaguered and ancient corner of the world, there existed someone like you, who was in fact you: a brave white woman who loved language and stories and true things (and who in that place where blacks were so loathed never forgot the truth that you were white). A brave white woman who loved true things and who decided, in the midst of a vicious war waged on black flesh, not to leave. Decided not to leave the country where the blacks were loathed and indeed treated like dirt: in fact far worse than dirt, and the whites mostly smiled upon it all, despite (or more often because of) truncheons cracked against black heads in the townships by white police officers, and teargas sprayed by them without care throughout places like Soweto, places like Boipatong, places like Sharpeville and Umlazi and Imizamo Yethu. The brave white woman who loved words and who was you didn't have to stay there in the (especially for blacks) beleaguered country—the place increasingly deplored by the entire world—and write about all of it: write about the blacks beaten and tortured in prisons, on the streets, and in their own homes; about the blacks and conscientious whites arrested and jailed without hope of a fair trial; about the famous black man who spent more than twenty-five years in prison, beaten and tortured, but who lived to become president, beloved throughout the progressive world; about the lies of the government; about the secret police; and more, and more. You didn't have to stay there in the *maelstrom*. And maelstrom it was, for couldn't they have done to you what they had done to one of the brave white men? To Albie Sachs? Bombed your car or home as they bombed his car in Mozambique, leaving him nearly dead and with one usable arm? Couldn't they have placed you under house arrest, as they had done to so many others? As had been done to others, your passport confiscated, your citizen's rights and privileges rescinded, your telephone tapped?

You never forgot, of course—and never let others forget—that whatever *could* have happened to you (but didn't) *would* have happened in far worse ways to black people, and did.

You didn't have to stay there and write, steadfastly, about *us:* about black people. About black people who, as your characters in all those novels and stories, were, like your white characters, complicated. Sometimes quixotic. Real. In doing so you did something monumental— monumental, yes—that very few white writers anywhere have ever done.

And perhaps, taking into account earlier intelligences communicated through other means, you already know this—but if you do not, or have forgotten, let me say it again, more openly this time: you are, in truth, one of the very few white people who has shown me—has really helped me believe—that white people can be more than just white. They can, from time to time, when they do their best, actually be human beings. White people, human beings: the concept is not actually oxymoronic. But what a tragedy that so many of us, with profoundly good reasons having to do mainly with history, would more often believe, correctly, that it is impossible for those two phrases ever to occur in the same sentence or have any relationship to each other.

And so if a brave white woman could risk her blood and limbs in that place so terrible because of what it did to blacks (in every way) *and* whites (mostly spiritually, sometimes physically) and all in between, could I, who also love language, do something brave as well?

Could it be possible to write the unwriteable? Write something about, for example, a man burned alive in Jamaica *in our time* because (so the work that was finally written seems to suggest) he loved—desired—other men?[1]

Could one write about men loving each other but also (literally) torturing each other? Write about the torment of intimate emotional cruelty, or the torment of (while manacled in some secret room) feeling lighted cigarettes stuck into one's testicles?

Could one write about the men-loving white men who hated blacks? About the black men who hated white men or—far worse—sometimes themselves?

And write about the black women who deeply loved black men and each other, and our children, but spat at men like me the acid-bile of the word *faggot*? ("Yeah, uh-huh. He a faggot. God*damn*. Ain't that some shit! Little ass-switching faggot!")

Remembering that you didn't leave. Nor flinch. Like some of the other brave ones of all colors, you stayed. Stayed there.

But please remember this once more, as I do: that when you said exactly what you said to me so long ago, expressed that belief in me in fact not at all so long ago, I knew then that you helped rescue—made even more possible—a young man's life. A young black man's life. A young black gay man's life: one in which very few other people were or had ever been interested. For who like you, doing all that you do and in your particular position, had yet taken the time, looking directly at me, to say those precious words—words like "Do this" or "You must do this" or "Make sure *that you continue to do this, so that at last someone—you—will have done it." Who, aside from you, so far away across the sea, writing your old and new words in the country where black people's heads were routinely cracked open by truncheons and their faces regularly sprayed with teargas, or worse? The country of rigged political trials, car bombings of progressive radicals, and more . . . the country, by virtue of its hatred and evil, in no way unique in this world.*

And so here is my faith—what has become my faith, a voice inside me whispered long ago. My faith partly because of you and those very few like you. Faith, here, where, against what might once have ended with a rope around my neck or a bullet in my brain, I will *stay. Stay, in order to do this. And do it again. And again.*

===

LORDE

But in fact this is not a poem
               Audre
                      it is not a
                      poem nor an
encomium nor anything like that anything
                         hagiographic   no not at all because I
                                   know I know now more than ever after
                        that book about you after
              Warrior Poet especially after it that
       you are not a
     goddess
as I foolishly (callowly) had once believed you to be
     not hagiography this is not but simply a
letter to you Audre: one that requires
                  white spaces on the page or not many white spaces because
well there is so much to say isn't there and not enough
   time not enough space to add up all the words of
     gratitude Audre for all of your   strength your
                              power and
            (Caribbean girl   *Eastern* Caribbean girl)
for all the years Audre of your saying and
                  articulating and
                     enunciating the
        unsayable   *the* unsayable   the
                  unspeakable   about
                     us about you about
     because this is who we are the crucial words let them be known and
       let us all and each be seen Audre heard and
         the sum of all the parts making the whole making the
         person making the
                 me

articulate it: black   and

Caribbean and man-loving and

all of it the sum of the parts making the whole and

before reading you before that declarative language Audre not knowing quite

that it was possible to be

black and

homo and

Caribbean and

Jamaican

and immigrant and

writing about it

naming it

across these geographies of

nation and self and

Kingston   the Bronx   Clarendon   Trafalgar Park   Aenon Town   Brixton

Norbrook   Emancipation Park   Mona   Treasure Beach   Hope Pastures   Harlem

and so thank you Audre for the language and the

manifold ways to say it and *know* it and   *feel* it, Audre   and

but no   no   this is not a poem, Audre

nor a damned encomium

it is merely a

(but how well you know it)

deep

oh let it be deep

calling

calling of your name

Audre

Audre woman

womanpoetvoice

voice and power   language that helped—that helped us—

Yes   :

BALDWIN

Dear Sir, Dear Father—

You came to me recently in a dream—indeed, many years after I first found you entirely on my own in a bookshop somewhere. In that time, long before the intimate dream, I considered you . . . but how to say? Not quite mine, I thought back then, though without question you always were. Back then, I found you elusive, sometimes elliptical: qualities which daunted and entranced me, and which maybe you had inherited from Mr. James, whose intricately layered novels you loved (as did and do I); or maybe they were passed on to you from the magisterial church, the cadences of which never left your deepest blood. You were just beyond my reach in those younger days, and possessed a knowledge at that time too terrifying (one of your favorite words) for me to occupy. That knowledge had been bitterly won by all of those who had come before us, and by you; it began with love and anger, and exploded with rage, and ended with love and anger. Yours was a rage that, for the longest time, I could not fathom (or refused to fathom), though I myself possessed it; it was a storm that I could not (would not) countenance, though its bloodfury crackled just beneath my skin, and especially beneath the skin of my more often than not smiling face: the sometime protection of the clown, or the coward, or the much-beaten child, or the presuicide, or the lunatic-psychotic, or the dreamer . . . or the man already dead. It was the fury of *To be black and conscious in America is to be in a constant state of rage*, you said, and *Father, teach me, I prayed, but please not so harshly, not with such rage* . . . but the bloodfury, yours and mine and all of ours, was, in the cauldron of America, unavoidable. (Coming from Jamaica, our island hearts did not, I know now, wish to learn that bloodlesson so soon.) And perhaps in denial of your anger—for it did scald, and scald again, with but a glancing look upon the page of your conjured worlds—I thought for some time, chose to believe, that *my Father—this one, the black American one—speaks from a profoundly different religious tradition than mine, and that is why he is so very angry: yea, for his is the African American sermonizing voice: that thundering and poetic richness that runs through his very American blood and which he would not have been able to escape even had he turned his flesh inside out and exposed it to one hundred suns, then turned it back on itself again. For black Americans* always *are*, I thought, *unlike Jamaicans, so very very angry* . . . the uninformed ruminations of an unexposed child. A child listening to *that voice*, I thought, *unmistakable, unerring in its reach, heard by one in barbershops and on street corners, in front of storefront churches and chicken-and-ribs joints alike, from Harlem to Memphis to Cleveland to KC to DC (especially Southeast) to American Beach to Decatur to Charlotte— and, God knows, onward to Chicago (try the South Side first), Gary, Detroit, and straight on back down to NO. You knew it, Father. Felt it. Inhabited and embodied it. But it was not mine. It was not—is not—the reserved, preserved formal poetry of my true-true people's Anglican church, heard in one hundred and more Jamaican country towns. It was the language of my black American cousins and my black American Father, and Father, we still scorned you all and yours then, did we not? We in the*

*archipelago thought ourselves better than you all in the US of
A, did we not? And as if all that were not enough injury to
egregious insult, Father, mark this: that no one—no one at all
in school, when I began formally to study you—ever, ever said
anything about you loving, needing, wanting other men.*

How could I have known then just how very much
I had always needed you? How much I would discover
how in fact I had always needed, so urgently, to love you?

You came to me recently in a dream. But all the
things you told me in the dream you had told me before, years ago. I remembered. Still, I needed you at the
time of this recent dream as I had needed you long ago
but had not known it. I needed you to tell me again all
that you had told me in dreams years before, so that as I
listened, I could feel your hand once again on my fore-
head, and your voice once again at the back of my throat:
your voice telling me once again, *Go on, go on, child. Do
it. Just* do *it. Yes, child, just go on. Don't wait for the fire. For
the flames will come as sure as Gabriel; as will the rage. Do not
wait. Just move. Move,* you said.

The only thing for which I have not forgiven you—
and for which I may never forgive you—is that you died.

Yes, you died. But you didn't leave me

Fatherless,

Father,

nor without brothers.

MORRISON

And so it was, Lady, that Someone offered you language:
offered it to you brilliantly, in a golden glove outfitted

with silk. A glove festooned not with glittering rubies (which, for your purposes and by your measure, might have been gaudy), but with pearls: quiet, understated, simple. Themselves. And from the sea. Pearls, the sea, very old voices, much memory, a listening, an attending. And so thenceforth out of the attending arrived Sula. And later Sethe. Paul D. Jadine, and Cholly. And Joe Trace, and Stamp Paid, and Guitar and Milkman and Ruth. One could never imagine a time when there would not be more from you, but that time will, we know, come. We know it as a dreaded fact, as one understands—knows—that one day one's most beloved will have to die—as will all of us. Yet the bounty of what has been imagined and offered on the page abides and endures. (Endures: for when Ms. Welty died—someone whose visions you have admired, as have I—in my case the correct word would indeed be loved—I thought, Well. Well, now. The truth is that the world ought to end just now, I thought. It should end as it ought to have ended when, in 1992, Ms. Lorde left this place. As it ought to have in 1987, when Mr. Baldwin left. But the world didn't, astonishingly, crumble when they departed . . . as it didn't, amazingly, when Ms. Welty moved on. Miraculously, it all will, all of it, somehow be all right. We have their words. The pages and the voices speaking out of them. Something survived, and survives still.)

And so it was, Lady, that something in your windings and byways on those pages reached out to that small boy in that place—that often not very nice place—very far from where you were, and told him, unquestionably, utterly confidently (and quietly, *softly*), that he too could do something along the lines of what you had done. Could at least do something that began with (but did not end only with) imagining. Through all of his lonesome hours, through each of his alone hours (often alone, for few around him wished to spend much time with a faggot then; few found much use, except to hurl stones or actual refuse at his head, for a faggot then), he wondered about them, those people: Pecola, Sula, Sethe, Paul D. . . . and about the ghost-daughter herself with her depthless black eyes and unlined hands. And all the others and the others and the others still. Where had they all come from, he wondered, and how had the Lady imagined them?—questions that pondering them, reading them, would not answer entirely, but would instead deepen—lengthen—over time. The depth and length could often be formidable. But if she could do it, he thought, that little brown boychild girl-eyed faggot, then maybe, *maybe*, he dared to think (but what a laugh! What a dreamer! So others in his world, had they known of his yearnings, would have snorted in his direction, even spat at him, over his ridiculous head)—just maybe, I could do it too. Someday. Somehow, he dared to think. Little ridiculous, pathetic, stupid faggot. Sitting there thinking. Dreaming. And reading. But keep it all to yourself, he thought, far from harmful hands and contemptuous eyes.

And so he read you for years, Lady. Read you with devotion. With the devoutness in the pursuit that was, for him, virtually prayer. (But also escape. God help him—help me, Jesus Lord, to escape.) And watched you.

Watched you carefully. Scrutinized you with a gaze as unstoppable as it was resolute. *The steel within.* He possessed it. The steel that one must possess when loathed.

He scrutinized the proud carriage of your shoulders and head: that gray head, increasingly gray and then dreadlocked across the years—that told the world that you, like those before you (and about whom more often than not you had written), had—have—dignity. Grace. *We* have dignity, irrespective of what the nations at large tell us, what the many scowls and curled lips at large tell us. We are possible. We who originally came from (no, were wrenched from, as one would rip out, with a clenched fist, the intestines of a still-living person) that place so long ago and across the waters. That place that is, that remains, both the flesh and the blood.

And so it is possible—in fact hugely necessary—to recount our stories. To remember them. To not have them languish among the many, the innumerable *disremembered and unaccounted for.* Do you remember? Language that lingered long afterward in the wake of a grieving ghost. *This is not a story to pass on. So rememory it,* he thought, using the word conjured out of the mouth of that needful ghost, and *re-member* . . . no matter how painful. No matter how many wish not to remember, and will not, and cannot. Remember if only because of all the pathetic little shit-faggots still lying broken-boned in darkened corners, sucking (if they are still alive) flame-blackened thumbs. Remember if only because of all the necks broken by hemp knotted and hung from trees, and the "fire-cooked blood" that you, Lady, wrote about. Remember the dead and dying children on scorched fields, the people screaming in black underground places with their hands cut off and their genitals singed, and the fact that so many of us everywhere still are not—cannot yet be, will not be for some time yet—safe. Remember because *I*, he thought. *Because I am*, he who became me thought. *Because I am one. One with all of them.* All of them who are—who will always be, and always must be—we.

AGAINST PRECIOUSNESS

"Precious": that was the word he used in a brisk moment of our lively conversation. Typically for him, he'd said it simply, briefly, with no affectation, no "precious"-ness, and with just the slightest trace of disdain curling the left corner of his mouth. The word itself, as it stepped so easily out of his mouth (a mouth that I had already decided, weeks ago when I'd first met him, to listen to closely, finding that he often said many interesting things, some of them very insightful—and usually, though not always, with an affable smile that encouraged deeper and more intimate interaction), unsettled me; for there we were, on a late-October Sunday afternoon whose pale sunshine would gradually turn to brisk, chilly rain in the early evening; we were speeding down the motorway from Cambridge to Essex (my first time on a British motorway, one of the fast A roads), on our way to the home of the great Guyanese novelist and intellectual Wilson Harris, whom I would finally have the opportunity of meeting, after years of wanting to do so, in about an hour's time, at the end of our drive, when we arrived in Chelmsford, where Sir Wilson had lived for decades. (Needless to say, the word "nerves" could hardly describe my feelings; but the story of my triumphing over the nerves, the sweaty palms, and the feelings of intense self-consciousness regarding excessive armpit perspiration, will be a story for another day. When I tell it, I'll also tell how, in spite of all that nervousness and shyness, it was finally possible to spend several enthralling and fully enjoyable hours in the company of the man who had not only been extremely kind to me on several occasions, but who had really been a type of literary *padrino*—the man whose work I had for years, in fact for more than a decade, found fascinating, abstruse, impenetrable, deeply mystical, poetic, incomprehensible at points, powerfully mythic, and, in short, simply among the most brilliant and formidable in twentieth-century Caribbean literature, in every way imaginable unlike anyone else's: Padrino Harris, to whom my traveling companion had on several occasions affectionately and correctly referred to as "the James Joyce of Caribbean literature." The story of our afternoon-into-evening spent in Padrino Harris's Chelmsford home, eating cookies ["biscuits"] and drinking coffee as he told his stories, should eventually be written, because one should always write a story after having met an elder, an ancestor, a *padrino*. You should tell what the entire experience was like, as you simultaneously recall the awe and the joy you felt in hearing his accent, still so distinctively Guyanese after so many years in England. But in the meantime you do have the memories and the photographs, and the nerve endings still crying, "Wake up! Wake up!" at the ends of your fingers.)

My traveling companion for the afternoon—the man hurtling us down the A road to Chelmsford, who had just used the word "precious" in regard to a writer whose work we both, for the most part, had liked (I'd actually really loved it, though I didn't know the more recent work as well as the earlier)—was (and as of this writing still is) a scruffy, bearded, eyeglassed, seventy-something, deeply energetic Cambridge lecturer emeritus whose mental peregrinations I had enjoyed hearing expressed almost from the moment I'd first met him at a conference on Caribbean poetry convened at the university just before the start of the 2012 Michaelmas term. During this afternoon's drive, he shared marvelous stories about Wole Soyinka, whose renowned testiness, combined with a justifiable impatience with the sort of Eurocentric arrogance common at Oxbridge, had permitted the suffering of very few fools during the brief period Soyinka had passed at Cambridge as a Visiting Fellow at Churchill College in 1973. My companion's hilarious recounting of some of the writer's chilly reactions to locally encountered pretensions and just plain rudeness will also be a story for another day.) The names of various other contemporary writers came up; and so when he used the word "precious" in reference to a writer whom many, myself included, would regard as supremely gifted, I drew up short.

"Precious?" I asked. "What exactly do you mean? What does that mean?" For while I sort of knew what I thought he meant, I wanted to know exactly what he really had intended to say.

"Well, some of [the writer's] more recent work has been a bit precious," he replied, his eyes narrowing as he kept them focused on the road. "A little new-agey . . . a little . . . *sincere*."

If you were paying close attention to his face and words just then, which I was, you would soon have become aware of what sounded like the faintest suggestion of a possibly deeply byzantine irony and wryness, as seemed to be the case also in his slightly lifted eyebrows. But what did that elusive "sincere" mean?

"Oh, you know," he continued, "it's like with Americans. They're always so *sincere*, aren't they? But I never believe them." I permitted the vast but amusing generalization (though I understood what he'd meant to infer) to pass, and listened carefully as he went on to say that he thought that the writer whom we were discussing had done himself a great disservice by moving farther away, literally and imaginatively, from the very evocative, powerful language traditionally used by the people in the poor community in which the writer had been born and raised: a language of specific culture and also class and even—especially—ethnicity. A language deeply imbued with its own highly specific, complex and complicating metaphors, intuitions, and allegorical intelligence, all of which had so illuminated and, according to my companion, enlivened the writer's earlier works. The writer now tended to "overwrite," my companion opined, and write *about* feelings rather than simply *show* feelings. (What I also heard in that remark, though my companion didn't actually use the word, was *risk*, as in a writer's work in risking the revelation of real, not contrived or clever, feelings.) The writer's more recent work, my companion felt, managed very skillfully in several instances, and with a sublime display of craft, to describe "the thing itself," without ever itself becoming "the thing"—which becoming might move closer, I suspected, to the achievement of true sublimity.

This persuasive assessment from someone whose mind and opinions I very much respected in regard to the more recent works of a writer whom I without question considered extraordinarily gifted deeply worried me. For the assessment seemed to suggest that the writer so capable of conjuring such gorgeous words that could move one to tears, as I had been moved—moved even to a place beyond tears—was traveling farther away from a primal source, in a sense, of brilliance and power: the brilliance and power in the language(s) of one's own culture, whose quotidian life also provided repeated opportunities to experience and journey through the ineffable: the realm of the mainly unremarked marvelous, really, in one's own particular everyday, that in my experience and also in that of the writer in question, had frequently, if not always, been overlooked, shunted aside, undervalued. The undervalued that, in my culture, contained the power of (for instance) a broad-backed, big-backsided black woman bending over a laundry basket, who as she straightened to hang all those clothes on the line and reap the benefit of the ferocious Jamaican sun, shouted in patois to her neighbor about some "wutless" man who did run off wid a gyal young enough to be him pickney, to rass. The power in what the toothless, poor, illiterate old man down the road (who could be—no doubt was—

someone's grandfather), the man who sits outside all day watching the world go by and whom nearly everyone in that small town refers to respectfully and sometimes playfully as "Daddy," knows, but also does not know— for in spite of the reverers and hagiographers who would seek to mythologize the likes of him, he is not infallible. Every old black person or village elder does not, in fact, possess infinite knowledge, and it is our job—among one of many of our jobs as writers—to search out that interior life with all of its disappointments and triumphs, and render it, not slavishly nor hagiographically, but faithfully—truthfully, vulnerably—on the page.

"But then why keep running when you're already riding the bus?" my companion remarked a moment later, quoting a Scottish friend. The comment sounded wise, commonsensical, and playful enough to swim in waters favored by West African (or Jamaican) proverbs. The Scottish friend had made the remark in regard to artists who had permitted themselves to be seduced, to varying not-good degrees, by the artist-consuming establishment at large: by the trappings and blandishments of prestige, fame, wealth, lionization (and all these courtships sometimes coming very early in a promising career); and by positions on the boards of prestigious institutions (such as some of those occupied by the writer in question) or many, many invitations to do many, many things that might take one away from the very thing that had once given one's writing that edge, that power, that unmistakable rawness: the I-don't-give-a-fuck-I'll-tear-your-heart-out sense of daring and risk that can make art so exciting, precisely because it fears nothing—not even (or especially not) its author.

That's not a bus that I want to ride—not ever. In fact, I don't ever wish to go anywhere near it. (No, not ever.)

I believe that my companion's words especially disturbed and even scared me precisely because I have spent what will soon be slightly longer than a complete calendar year here in Cambridge's extremely rarefied (to say the least), powerfully seductive environment, that reeks (to say the least) of elitism: a nearly if not actually mythic place of legendary and actual privilege and power, for which some people would slice open their mother's carotid with nary a second glance nor even a sigh in order to gain access. Access to the ultimate citadel. To Valhalla. And to be sure, the sheer beauty of the place can get to you; for it is without question magnificently beautiful. Some, myself included, would say mythically gorgeous. But still. For its great beauty aside (a beauty that, especially in its vaulting and imposing architecture, also illustrates, among many other things, man's profound lack of humility and delusions of grandeur; accent very heavily there on "man"), it is an environment that, for all its intellectual richness and the breadth and depth of its manifold offerings (and many of those offerings, though often staid, are sometimes, in the most surprising quarters, also rich, profoundly moving, and heart-filling: deeply *human*, in short), nonetheless in the main occupies a terrain worlds away from the languages and people that have always thrilled me the most, fascinated and mesmerized me, and provided my imagination—I hope—with the "edge" that I wish never to lose nor feel is in any way simply not present, not *alive* and *there* and beating, *breathing*, in whatever it is that I've written. As fascinating as this time at Cambridge has been, I know that it—or someplace else like it—can never truly be my home: not my home, though other people who look like me might find it more possible to snuggle in between the colleges' cold stones upon which, across the imperial centuries and before them, so many monarchs' glorified feet have trodden. (Indeed, some people who come from my corners of the world might even find it the ultimate achievement to wind up either permanently directly *between*, or permanently as one *of*, those cold, implacable stones.) Even as these thoughts rolled through my head in the wake of my companion's remarks, I found myself reflecting on—and once again internally experiencing, as if replaying recordings in my head—the mercurial, acrobatic language that I had long ago absorbed into my bloodstream in the Bronx, in Kingston: the languages and intonations of those people who, in the eyes of many and at times perhaps especially so in the eyes of some individuals whom I have met this year, would be "those people": anthropological specimens sometimes regarded as interesting and exotic, even inventive ("They are marvelously inventive with their music, aren't they?" I could imagine some individuals whom I have come to know this year saying), but ultimately of scant importance when placed alongside the Titans of Western "civilization." (At least we know now that the word "civilization" simply must be placed within quotation marks when using it to refer to those who, in the name of what they have so doggedly defined as their "civilization," have torn out the throats of virtually every people they have encountered since they themselves first crawled out of the northern primordial slime.)

And so maybe, I began to think more rapidly and furiously, maybe that's where what my companion called "preciousness" begins for some people: in the place where one awakens in the morning and forgets that the armpits have always had a foul smell when one awakens— a markedly intense one, in fact, until they've been thoroughly washed. And even then they might still stink. Yes, I thought: preciousness could begin in the place where (but God forbid) one forgets that the asshole will also have and has always had a strong smell, an odor of which one will be particularly aware upon awakening if—in groggy curiosity, in boredom, or in the simple but deeply private desire of wishing to savor the forthright power of your own stench—you rub your fingers there, and sniff them. The smell is not casual, it is yours, and preciousness will insist that you forget all about it; that, no bad pun at all intended, you leave it behind. It will insist that you forget the smell of your unwashed crotch as well: ripe, rank, your own reliable stink. The stink that haunts used underwear, occasionally leaves itself in deepest pleasure on the tongue of an uninhibited lover, and slinks with and without shame through fetish-sex personal ads.

Preciousness will of course eschew the piss-reeking Bronx subway stations through which, unfazed and calmly accustomed, one spent many years of life walking. Preciousness would instead prefer that one forgets what that piss smelled like, what it felt like and might feel like still to walk through its reek, and what the faces of the other people who have to live daily with that reek, because they've no choice, look like. It will be all the more unfortunate if you purposely forget what that stench smelled like, because (yes, you guessed it!) purposeful forgetting makes all the more possible the entrée and ascendancy of preciousness.

And in fact each of these smells—and of course arguably the most potent of them all, that of shit—are smells that I associate with (though not only with) the so-called "third world," and with my own corner of it, Jamaica: smells that I associate with poverty and deprivation, more often than not, but also with life: with real life that, like death, life's other Janus face, is utterly precious, but never—for me, at least—in any way "precious." Smells that are of and from the body, one's own body and the bodies of others, obviously contribute to this enormous thing that we call life. (Considering the inevitability of strong and even foul smells in life, it would be true to say that Chaucer was in *no way* precious in his writing.) And although I honestly cannot say that I'm particularly fond of the smell of shit (not yet, anyway; it's not a smell that I find particularly welcoming or easy to deal with, with equanimity, for extended or even brief periods), I acknowledge its presence and necessity, whether by way of a man squatting to void his bowels over a small hole in the sidewalk early one morning on lower King Street in downtown Kingston, to the outrage of some nearby

pedestrians and early shopkeepers, or by way of the powerful fecal stink left behind in a public toilet at Trin-
ity College, Cambridge, by one of the college's black-
gowned fellows, with whose stomach the meal he had so
heartily consumed only a few hours before had clearly
not agreed.

And then finally, of course, there's the part that draws
one up even more abruptly, enabling one to see, vis-à-
vis preciousness, what is obvious and was obvious from
the start: that preciousness ultimately is gooey. It's the
fakery and cheapness of not-life itself; a refusal to engage
with what, in our violent, glorious, detonating, and ever-
renewing world, our world of geopolitics and constant
scrabbles for power and dominion, so undeniably *is*. It's
the cloyingness of saccharine compliments or small talk,
as well as a quietly psychopathic reluctance to admit that
belches and other expulsions do, like it or not, exist.

And what did I learn from all this, from these
thoughts and the conversation, as we continued speeding
through the pale-skinned afternoon down the A road to
Chelmsford and the home of the great Guyanese writer,
and afterward? Perhaps only what I had known, at least
intuitively, all along: that there was no way in hell that
a year in an exalted, mythically beautiful place, and all
of its tacit enticements to disregard the world *out there*,
not so far from King's Parade, could in any way ever
move me to step away from my Jamaican and Northeast
Bronx languages—languages of my blood—nor from the
people who, whether they often infuriate me or not,
will always be irrevocably mine; that preciousness be-

comes deplorable—unconscionable—when it seeks to ignore human suffering and atrocities, such as (for example) Israel's latest bombing of Gaza: the wholesale slaughtering of an untold number of Palestinians by the Israeli military, occurring right now, as this essay is being written in November 2012; and that, for an artist who really wants to maintain proximity to the important elemental stink of his own armpits and other bodily areas, constant vigilance against the delights, cuteness, patness, and sheer falseness of preciousness is required. In this regard, I believe that it greatly helps for one to recall as often as possible, in every sense, not only where one intends to go—hopes to go—but also where one has come from: in my case very much from people whose still-breathing bodies were routinely thrown overboard from suffocating ships into the cooler but unfortunately uncomforting sea, whose necks were efficiently snapped by taut ropes, and whose flesh was incinerated by flames whose crackles, as the dangling body twitched and blazed, produced a very different stink. People who, across the centuries, were forced to admit into their bodies the engorged parts of those who owned them for centuries. There, one's own infinite and deeply personal catalog of memory against the ultimately offensive, dishonest, precious stink and artifice of preciousness.

INTERVIEW WITH THE NOT-POEM

Interviewer: But how can you call yourself
a "not-poem"?

You look, from all appearances,
like a poem.

You crouch,
shuffle,
swing and sway
and arrange your lines,
syllables,
metaphors and similes
like a poem.

Your outside parts
resemble that of a poem,
of all poems,
as do all your other parts.

So how,
pray tell,
can you not be a poem?
Explain if you will
this "not-poem"-ness,
this state of *un*.

Not-Poem: But then do not call me a poem,
for no, I am not one.

Thomas Glave

I came recently from that country
(about which by now you surely will have heard)
in which it was most unwise,
ungood,

simply *un*,
to be a poem.

Entire poems were murdered
in silent fields.

Stanzas,
though begging for their lives,
their limbs,
were strung up
and destroyed.

Delicate lines
and vulgar ones,
those both insensitive to light and fond of it,
and even mere epithets,
cries in ignorance and mediocrity,
simple daily failure
but also joy,
were torched,
leaving only ashes,

bare ashes,
in their wake.

Erased unto oblivion.

Scratched out of paper villages,
books unimaginable.
Books that, though outlawed,
were somewhere dreamt.

The smell of burning poem flesh,
rancid, sooty
and profane,

shrouded entire cities,
coastal plains.

Poem conversations were spied on
by poem-despising agents,
and entire towns of poems
emptied,
laid waste.

Rounded up and deported.
Torched, as I said.
Stoned.

So no, do not call me a poem.
I will never be a poem again.

Interviewer: But still, you do look much like a poem,
and sound like one.
You smell—

Not-Poem: But then you know nothing, I see,
of the flags that, in that time, so swiftly, were raised.
Raised within days.

Yes, raised over twenty million roofs,
hoisted high over one hundred million TV antennas.

Flags, proud flags.
Flaggery everywhere.

Thomas Glave

Flags raised against poems
and those who resembled them.

Flags sprouted in airports.
Especially in airports.

At all security points,
and all customs checks.
Proof of citizenship so critical,
fealty more so.

But flags too in previously bland shopping malls,
and across yawning suburban lawns.

Poems dared not walk unaccompanied to the market,
nor—no, not ever—to worship
in poem holy places.

Poems were wrenched off planes
by those too edgy to fly with them.

"Who knows, they could be one of them!" some shouted,
teeth bared but shoulders cowering—
rocks in their dreams,
if not yet in their hands.

For—yes, did you not know?
Poem-children began ducking stones at school,
and more than one poem
(or anyone who looked like one)
was felled by bullets.

Bullets—
the good old-fashioned kind that still served.

Better than the national pastime, and more to the point.

Bullets still good enough to bring down a dirty poem,
to blow the heads off poem motherfuckers
who should anyway have had the sense,
long ago,
to go back where they came from.

Dirty poems,
cocksucking poems,
poems that didn't speak the language,
that chattered only in an outlandish gibberish.

Poems that stole jobs
and their dreams,
those elusive dreams.
The dream.

Poems that flooded the nation, bred like rabbits.
Poems that fucked with life as they knew it.

Poems that prayed too much or too little,
always with those awful accents,
that savage garb.

Poems without flags,
the flag.

Bullets urged on by flags
that stated, loudly,
This is who I am, and what I believe.
And you, they asked, *who are* you?

Interviewer:	Do you actually expect us to believe—
Not-Poem:	Only that I am a not-poem.
	Not a poem.

Thomas Glave

Interviewer: But you have said that flags were used to—

Not-Poem: Oh, but let me tell you.
They, they believed in their flag—
its supposed nobility, its invincibility.

Is not a flag
(though it may blare, loudly enough, its share of red)
easier to gaze upon, caress,

than one million and counting scorched hands in a field?

Than sixty million legs and limbs suspended
between branches, leaves?

Than two hundred thousand eyes peering outward
from crouching hoods?

Than deserts baked with dead poems
and with fingers, knees?

A flag doesn't answer back, after all.
It makes no pretensions to having a right to its own life.
It couldn't care less about hunger, or thirst.
It loves bombs, which inform the songs
droned out, routinely, in its name.

It drapes coffins at will, and with grace.
And most of all—yes, most important—
it adores histories that never were,
that were never taught,
nor known,
and will never be.
Not-histories.

Interviewer: And so the poems—

Not-Poem: In that place,
                   the poems ran to the hills and hid.
                   "All bets are off," someone said,
                   "only not-poems will live now."
                   That is what they said.
                   And so we transformed ourselves—
                   yes, our faces
                   and our hands.

                   We quickly grew six fingers
                   and three eyes.

                   We covered our mouths
                   with clever lines from novels
                   penned by dilettantes.

                   We made the stanza
                   merely a memory,
                   while retaining allegory.

                   We scaled the walls
                   where freedom, once advertised,
                   no longer stretched.

                   We ceased worshipping
                   in all the poem holy places.

                   We replaced God
                   with the flag,
                   for freedom's sake.

Thomas Glave

Interviewer: And so now you—

Not-Poem: Now
I am a not-poem,
still fearful of bullets,
uncertain of my lines,

content with no plot—
the plot they were certain,
beneath their flag,
we all possessed—

their darkest dream,
a poem. Any poem.

The unending line.

(Interview conducted in late September–early October 2001, USA)

THE BODY
AND ITS CONFLICTS

MEDITATION ("ON BAREBACKING")

===

Because now this is it, what we both want: me inside him, him inside me. What we want: to go into each other this way, completely unsheathed. "Unprotected." To feel, really *feel*, the movements that some would term "dangerous," even "deadly": the sensation of ourselves moving through each other without fear. Without shame. Without (yes, at last, after so many years of so many warning messages, decades of Do-Not-Do-This-or-Ye-Shall-Pay-the-Dire-Price messages) worry. Without anxiety—for the world with all its disapproval and warning is *out there*, we now tell ourselves, *so leave it behind. Forget about it. Yes, forget it*, he repeats to me, as, in this darkness that is utter secrecy and little more than breath and flesh, flesh and desire, I feel myself, an "outlaw" but truly free, now again rocking above him, pushing behind him; breathing in, out; moving into him now deeper, harder; my hands grasping his back; my arms reaching around to hold him closer; my mouth seeking again that part of his flesh (the taste of him still in my mouth, the width of his fully exposed length still filling my throat); my hand reaching down to steady myself inside him—just there, then there again, then even deeper, before the *And can we go even deeper?* part that leads to the *Yes, of course, because* part . . . which is exactly what I want, exactly the place I want so much to be: where I am right now and wish to remain, without hesitation or remorse, without warnings or scoldings as, a little later, or perhaps sooner than I expect, I will feel him doing the same to me. For he too will think and feel these things. He too will curl his lip at all those remembered warnings about "safety" as, unimpeded by clear barriers or the constant admonitions of Those Who Know Best, he will move, rock, twist, and thrust in that place that is mine, his bare flesh against mine: here, where, in secrecy, we can remain, but also become. Remain together unmolested, at least for now ... Remain, our faces turned toward each other's and occasionally away from each other's; our faces sweating, perhaps spasming; our faces portraying, among other words, the words "Yes" and "Yes, entirely," as, beyond here, we disclose absolutely nothing to anyone of this union that is, because of what and how it is, "illicit." Nothing will be disclosed to any of the skulking frowners always outside, the knit-browed judges ever present out there. The stalwart purveyors of the *Do Not* and *You Should Not* rhetoric. *You really should know better by now*, they will say, *for haven't we all lived and died with It, the terrible thing, for how many decades now? Haven't we learned? Haven't you learned? Don't you know that you should not be so* (and then, as always, comes the dreaded word—the resented word) Irresponsible?

But then clearly some of these words, and the tone in which they have been repeated to us over the years, form one of the irritations here, the vexations. Irritation, even fury, over years of being talked at and case-managed.

Years not only of our having had to be "careful," but also of being commanded, *berated* by The Authorities, to be so. Years of being told by The Authorities that we are Bad because we might choose, for whatever reasons (such as the pursuit of our own particular joining, a need with its own winding history), not to be "careful." All the years of having to navigate between obstacles to unimpeded closeness—the closeness we and others have craved for so long. And so perhaps partly in defiance of "reason" and everlasting caution (what tenacious caution, to abide not merely for years, but for decades!), here we are today and every day being Irresponsible, this man and me; being Irresponsible perhaps because we care deeply for each other, or do not; but in any event doing what we are doing right now because—well, because it feels *good*. It feels good unwrapped and gripped fearlessly in the hands, it brings real bliss sliding uncovered between the teeth, and should I now tell you? Tell you how utterly amazing it feels to be able to say at last after years of *Be Safe* admonitions that here, at last, I am in that place of his without anything, anything at all wrapped around me, binding me. I am there without anything keeping him from feeling all of me, and he is, you are, *feeling* me in that deepest place from which now, holding onto me, pulling me down closer to you, into you, you murmur *Jesus* and *God* as I move, move myself in that place, your place, now completely unprotected, completely—

But yes. Exactly. Completely without shields.

Unshielded as, soon, I know, you will do it to me too. You will turn me around and say to me, whisper, *Stay*

there. Yes, and relax, you will say, while you—(but astonishingly slowly, in spite of the fervor that you feel), as I—(yes,
in exactly the way I have done so many times before).
Because really "This," we might say to each other and
even to The Authorities one day if provoked enough,
"This is what we want": not merely the moving inside,
but also what many consider the truest danger in every
sense: the releasing. The releasing at the moment of the
drawn breath and shudder that makes for the quick heat
that conjures "life," people say and believe, "life"—but
life that, at least in our time, can also lead to death. Death
so innocuously jetted between, or directly into, the place
of solid muscles, and carried forward from there. Inward.

Yes, of course we know. For a very long time now,
like countless others, we have known.

We know, and still are far from being the only ones.
Far from being the only ones who yearn, in spite of all
the risks, to move through each other without blockades.
To move without guilt . . . for once without guilt. Guilt
over being the despised "outlaw," and then survivor's
guilt: recalling all those who fell along the way and still
are falling, while we, in spite of all the risks, somehow did
not fall, have not fallen. *Not yet*, we do not say to each
other—and, we hope, privately, not ever.

But then what about the rest of it? The fact that of
course, in spite of everything that he tells you and has told
you, he still might give It to you; as he fears, though also
privately, that in spite of everything you have already said
and not said to him—assurances, promises, and pledges
of "the truth" openly uttered and tacitly understood—

you might give It to him. The possibility of "giving" in either direction a topic that, like a few other things, we have chosen not to discuss at length, as we remember that common sense and ultimate reality are generally rarely enjoyable. As unenjoyable as uncertainty and anxiety; the lingering pall of distrust. And fear. For always, no matter what we say or what we feel, what we occasionally term "the enemy"—enemy of life, love, desire, and the uninhibited pleasure that is truest freedom—is never that far away. Never far from our memory. Even if, as we might choose to believe, the enemy does not skulk directly between us, it always broods somewhere: *out there* somewhere and somewhere within: brooding and biding in the blood vessel; in the capillary that, so easily, unobtrusively, might rupture upon entry. We ponder these concerns now and again as (perhaps foolishly, even stupidly), determined to feel each other's *her*eness, we proceed into the practiced regularities of *relax, lie back,* and *Of course, everything will be fine*: words we mouth to each other and ourselves . . . remembering that such words have accompanied innumerable others to efficient and devastating communication of the enemy; to the disfigurings of pain and tragedy, when all so many wanted was simply pleasure, communion, and (yes, don't shrink away, *say* it!), what we want, in spite of everything: love.

Love, and so much more. And so now thinking of love; thinking of you and how much I want to feel you and keep you here beside me, inside me as I keep myself inside you where the muscles grip tightest and move myself more deeply there and *there*, I say again what we have never dared say aloud to anyone: that, in this moment, I simply *do not care*. I do not care about all that we have feared and continue to fear, because I am tired of all the enemy-laced years. Exhausted from all the years of public service announcements and precautions of Do not do this or that, Avoid contact with this, and Now make sure to don this carefully, so carefully, before you ease in, before you permit the easing in. Remembering all that death and shame and fear, but also so much yearning and desire, how can I not say right now that with this man (you), or with another, with *someone*, what I have always most deeply craved was, *is*, that closeness. Presence. Feeling. Touch. The joy and thrill of being seen, and seen, wanted. Being wanted: not at all easy to experience in this world, not so common—*and so now more than anything*, we say, you and I, *I want to feel myself inside you, completely uncovered. Feel myself up against you as you thrust against me. Here, where no one's brow will furrow in judgment, no one's lip curl in scorn, I want to tighten my arms around you and tell you these things: perhaps call you things like "beautiful one" or even "_____" (the most private name of all, never to be written). In this secrecy that blots out all unwelcome things (including certain truths), we might finally believe that desire and even love are . . . possible. Possible, because everyone ultimately wants to be desired and loved, loved somehow, isn't that right? That is what the world tells us. It is what popular songs and movies tell us we ought to want (though still mostly only with the faces and voices of men and women saying these things to each other—not too much, yet, with our kind, although it is beginning). If we do not admit that we want this and more—*

much more—we are kidding ourselves. Lying to ourselves. We know this, and in all honesty how could I not now admit that I am lonely without that touch and the gaze that looks at me and actually sees . . . me. As I would like to see you. You who are sometimes beautiful, I would like to say, *gorgeous, in fact, and* (whether or not this is true) *mine. Mine,* I would love to say, *underneath me, or above, or somewhere in between. And so give yourself to me. Open up and let me be there without interference. Without the obstacle of clear but durable barriers. Let me have an* effect *on you and make you remember me. Let me look at you and feel that I have touched you irrevocably in the most receptive place imaginable, and that now, more than ever— not only because of this, and because of so much more—you feel that way about me. As I—as you—*

But the truth is that I have no idea at all what will happen next. Nor does he. Nor might any of the other hes who may or may not traverse this terrain. I have closed my eyes. We have closed our eyes. Closed our eyes in part to the past—a past that gradually, amid laughter, discovery, love, and suffering, became terrible, unbearable, splotched by purple marks and relentless mutating encroachments. Splotched by shallow breathing, the thick scent of lilies, and the inhibition—corruption—of pleasure. Today, in the secret place and beyond it, we only know that the future, like death, like the most unforeseen outcome of risk, is unknowable. Today, at least, there will be no room for the publicly encouraged "good"-ness; no quarter for the commonly demanded "responsibility"; no place—not here, certainly—for the generally expected "maturity." Today, at least, life, joy, power, vulnerability, recklessness, desire, and perhaps the possibility of love and closeness (or at least the prospects of wanting and being wanted) loom. By way of the words that will later lead us to those deeper corridors of our dreams, the dream, we know now that, through these moments, our eyes remain closed, screwed tightly shut as, feeling this, then feeling that and that again, we shudder because he (you) will not let me go. *I will not let him go. Because now he is holding that part of me before his face and breathing it in. Because now, utterly unprotected, he is trembling and gasping beneath me, above me, calling out my name. He whispers it, shouts it, as I hold on to his hair, as he holds my hair, as we are not safe, no, in no way are we being safe. For there is, can be, no safety here, we both laugh. Anywhere. And so all right then, we say without saying it: Let it all remain a secret. One that we will never tell anyone, not this time nor when it happens again. For it will, we know, happen again. And again. But for now, we will keep silent, both of us, as we begin to dream. Dream of how, together, we are completely inside, unseen, where none of the others will ever find us. Where no one can stop us. Neither stop nor prevent us, my love, about which I promise—yes, to you I truly do promise—I will never, ever tell.*

Regarding Thoughts of (_____)

===

Fortunately, in order to save face and keep oneself from feeling terribly overexposed, while continuing the pretense that nothing is ever really wrong, everything is always really (of course) perfectly all right, it *is* finally possible to state from the start that one isn't at all the one writing this. It's not the author of the other words in this book now writing these words, now saying No: No, you think, insist, though you're still afraid; really afraid, actually. But again No, you tell yourself quietly: not this time. You really will keep yourself from going there this time, though resistance is hard—hard and sometimes near-impossible, it seems, when you feel most alone, when you're aware that the reality is in fact that you're alone. Face it, what you know in that most secret, most protected place: that you don't know anyone, really, with whom you can truly speak about this. But thank God for the hotline. Jesus, yes! Thank God for it, hell yes, and for their twenty-four-hour service.

And so as you continue writing this (keeping in mind all the while that you're not really the person writing this), remember that you should admit also that those other feelings never feel good: loneliness, isolation. Occasionally worse. And of course it's unnerving to talk about such things (which is why it's great that *you're* not talking about them), because really, when do black men ever talk about such things? When do we ever say or feel that we can possibly say things like: This can all be extremely difficult, in fact frightening; friends (or "friends"), even those who consider themselves really close friends, don't know (of course not—you'd never tell them), and even if they did know, they wouldn't understand, or, more likely, wouldn't wish to understand, since the subject does scare people, it causes them to back away. The way in which the world is set up, the worlds you mainly know and inhabit, anyway, makes it clear that middle- and upper-middle-class white people are permitted to speak about and actually feel these feelings, but not anyone not in those groups, and certainly not black men of whatever social class. One simply isn't allowed: not we who play basketball or soccer and who generally excel at sports or certain forms of music and dance; not we who sport gold teeth and gold chains and are (so some people say) generally very loud and sometimes—often—a bit fearsome in public. Not we of the enormous ever-ready cocks, who possess no interior lives whatsoever: no realm of the contemplative, no terrain of quietness and reflection. We are not allowed, nor do we allow ourselves, to say things like, *I've often thought about killing myself*, or, *But really sometimes cutting the wrists does seem like the only way out of all this, out of whatever's causing pain and grief and real misery at the present time. At least in death there might not be any feeling, or so some of us have been led to believe.* (But I've never been sure that I believe this.) *In death it would all be over, some of us have been led to believe, and that would feel so good, finally, so good to have it all finally be over.*

And of course I'm one of those black men—one of those people—who doesn't want to think about any of this either. I don't want to think about how this morning I thought No, I'm absolutely not going to do it today: not going to do it in spite of—because of—the recurring feeling, the really bad one, that confirms with an awful sinking that things are pretty sad right now and have been sad for a long time—and although they'll of course eventually improve, because everything does eventually in one way or another get better, it's very difficult, so bogged down this morning, to see or in any way believe in that down-the-road truth. Things feel all around thin and just not at all possible in any way, anywhere, just now, and feeling like this, when everything is so blurred and when breathing itself is asphyxiating, who wouldn't feel that intimacy, trust, and real caring with close friends is just impossible—is, in fact, completely unattainable? The simple truth remains: that the world is made up of those who are warmly married and those who aren't, those who are lovingly coupled and those who aren't, and for those who aren't, intimacy and sustained love are rarely spied creatures. The "rarely spied" part adds to the general difficulty.

While you know that it's never easy to jettison the bad feelings—unfortunately they never just *go away* like that—it can definitely help to try and move away from the sadness and the wanting so much to end it by working toward a wider, broader channel: the work that one tries to do as best as one can in the world, that involves generosity and compassion for others in the world, for the big wide world itself, and finally also for oneself. Even though you continue to feel this deep thing within that often really hurts, and gnaws, and makes you want to obliterate yourself, all you really need do in the hardest moments is just *try* to turn your gaze outward for a minute to that world out there, that one: the world so much in need. The world in which a great many people remain in dire need of a great deal of this and also that; the world in which bombs help no one, and in which water is best drunk and given to children when not chemically contaminated. The world in which it would indeed be nice to find at least one cup of milk this afternoon for all the children if only in just this one place where the milk is really needed, to say nothing of all the other places where providing just a cup of milk—although that would be a huge "just"—feels like emptying out the ocean with a teaspoon. This is the same world, everyone's, in which you hope, really hope, that all the people attempting to reach Europe from Senegal this time, trusting their lives and fates to a long pirogue bound northward across the hostile Atlantic by way of the Canary Islands, reach Spain, reach France, and do not simply all drown. When the bad feelings come, as they will, it's good to try as hard as possible in spite of the asphyxiating feeling to remember that one exists in the big broad world with a great many parched farmers today praying for rain, with who knows how many families praying for no onslaught of malaria this year (nor typhoid, nor cholera, nor meningitis), with it's-impossible-to-know-how-many-prostitutes   praying for a hospital—a cleaner one, this time—filled with what had never been common before: kind, sympathetic, giving hands. Though it's never easy when the bad feelings come, it will always be important to look if at all possible out to the big broad world, not inward to the searing one. In the big broad world, you'll remember that torture survivors, squinting, sometimes do manage to crawl up into daylight from blood-crusted subterranean chambers (a few of them, the men, mostly, still have all of their fingernails, and scorched flesh only above their groins, not below); as entire towns flee in fear of yet more ethnic cleansing: in flight from the stench of incinerated flesh which makes the youngest children vomit even as they flee, and creates the strangely reddened skulls, so many skulls glowing like embers, which unsettle everyone. The world, a good deal of it, sundered, scorched. The world that in spite of every choking feeling and the hands that want to pull you down to *drown, come down to drown*, remains yours and mine. Ours. That world, not yet finished, and still vital. Still here.

As, astonished, on some of the worst days, you think: I'm still here. A miracle. Here because of (although how is it possible, having recently felt something so completely different?) a renewed and recurring desire for life, for its frequent lights and surprises—absolutely, and also of course for its sorrow. (The always-rule, as everyone knows, being that no one can have some of it—life— without getting all of it, unless they die very young.) And so gradually you realize that it can be possible, though never guaranteed (since the bad feelings are very good at pounding poisoned blood deeply into the brain), to draw your attention away from the bridge from which privately, very quietly, you recently envisioned what would have been an easy enough, in fact even unremarkable jump: pedestrians and bikers rarely use that bridge, so you would have had privacy; and the waves so far below had looked calmly beckoning, and above all calming—like a blessing, really. A blessing, of course, because there's real peace down here, they'd quietly told you and might tell you again: calmness, although there will be intense coldness too, if you jump in any season other than latest summer or early autumn. The coldness will eviscerate you and make things unpleasant, but only briefly. And then at last quiet, oh quiet: finally a great deal of nothing but dark and quiet.

Things become a bit more hairy, of course, when you seriously start to imagine how you might best go about it. More hairy because then you know for certain that, fantasies and daydreams aside, you're really moving closer to doing it. But then it really helps when you at last decide on the method that you'll use for certain, because then you can finally relax and tell yourself, Terrific, I finally know, and so now I'm done. Now all I need to do is decide on exactly when and where, and whether or not I'll leave a note, and what to do about all the other last-minute things that may come up. But then what about that magnificent feeling of *peace* that you get when you finally know—isn't it incredible? It's really like nothing you've ever known—remember it? And it's only then that you know for sure that what you've heard said for years is true: that when people who want to do this at last reach clarity about how they'll go about it, their demeanor completely changes. All the pain and stress ebbs away. You're free, resolved, and as far as this world is concerned, you don't matter. You simply no longer matter, because from this point forward you no longer really exist.

Until that moment, of course, you've got to grapple with all the logistical questions: what would be the best way in terms of ease, least pain, speed, etc.? The questions that aren't so pleasant, like: If I fire this pistol that no one can know I have access to into my mouth, will the pain be so excruciating that I will feel it, though ideally I should die instantly, for a few horrible seconds before I do die? If I swallow all of these pills (the least scary way, though nothing about this can ever be not scary; but let's call it what it sort of is: a "gentler" way, recommended by several people), will I wake up thwarted as others have, in a puddle of my own acid-bitter vomit? But then the fact is that opening up the wrists in the bathroom should be easy enough, though visually unnerving: but still, little drama, and quick enough if you do it properly. (Make sure to do it *properly*.) Just some quick but careful slashes (they must be precise and deep in the particular way that will destroy the veins from which the blood, upon the veins' rupture, will immediately flow fastest) and then unfortunately (but not for long) the nausea-inducing redness in the warm water that you should have waiting in the sink to receive your warmth. It will be over soon enough. You'll be there in front of the sink on your knees, your apartment (or at least the bathroom) will be completely dark, so that you can't see what you're really, actually doing; and not a single person you know will know (your phone is turned off)—because of course if any of them knew they would try to stop you. In all likelihood, since you live alone and aren't particularly close to anyone—not with anyone who would check on you after a few days if they didn't hear from you—no one will discover you for days. But that won't be your concern. Discovery of the dead, and even or especially suicides, will always be the harsh task of the living. And it will be there, in that blessed and calming darkness, on your knees on the hard tile before your cool white bathroom sink, that, thanks offered up for the last time, you'll begin to feel yourself drifting away, drifting slowly but quickly away, from all of them: faces, names, and then the voices, gradually more distant. *And now here at last is a thorough and lasting punishing and erasing of the self,* you can think, *the punishing and erasing you've been wanting and waiting for since forever. Maybe since you were born. An erasing of the self that is the freedom to vanish.* And then, just that quickly, you'll be gone. You *will* be gone.

And that's exactly what the thoughts were like, wasn't it? Were like when you got very close, closer than you ever would have thought possible that time—remember? The thoughts moving like currents running through your hands that felt like blood, that felt like *Die,* like *Dying will be a* good *motherfucking thing today. A good thing to fix all the bad, all the can't-get-rid-of bad. The horrible-ugly bad, the kind of bad that rips out the throat and fucks you so hard way up in the ass like a real bitchcunt that you can't even talk about it bad. The kind of bad that deep down, deep, deep, makes you want to scream and throw yourself off the fucking bridge, it hurts so much. That kind of bad. And even then you can't talk about it. You can't talk about how it just makes you want to cut yourself up, carve yourself up, rip yourself into one million pieces. You can't talk about how it's really partly very much about hate, because hate forms the deep kernel of what hurts so bad, bad way deep down inside there. That's the hate that makes you want to explode yourself. To fire that gun off into your mouth. It works with rage. And the rage is cold. People might think it's hot, but they don't know. It's not hot and never has been. It's utterly cold, colder even than death, and it makes you want to kill, to murder, starting with yourself. Your pathetic, ridiculous, utterly extinguishable self.*

But fortunately I'm not the one writing this—so I can step away from whichever revelations disclosed herein seem to have disclosed too much, feel as if they careened much too close to the very personal bone, the most private secret bone about which one never ever speaks with anyone—not with *anyone.* I'm someone who writes, and all that precedes has been writing and is written—so now, breathing calmly, I can write something like: as it happened, the person who wrote all that and felt all that didn't die after having tasted those thoughts and having chewed on those feelings that hurt so much. He should have, but he was lucky that time. It may have been just simple fear that saved him that time, lucky bastard (or poor bastard, depending on how you look at it). Fear of pain, I'd say. Fear of what that pain would have really felt like in the opened wrists after a minute or two; fear of what that bullet would have really felt like ripping into the brain just before everything went permanently quiet.

(And here's a little secret, a scary one: a cousin of the person who wrote about all those feelings took his own life. He shot himself in the chest, that cousin, right in the heart, the evening of the day that he heard in court, at the conclusion of a terribly acrimonious divorce, that he would not be granted custody of his two sons . . . one of whom, he had definitively learned not long before, was not his biological own, but his best friend's. And so he went home that evening and, just like Richard Cory in the poem, fired off a pistol into himself. *He* was the one none of us in the family had ever even vaguely considered might do such a thing: an impossible idea. Outlandish. Simply not part of his makeup. Maybe he wouldn't have done it, some people said, if he had remained in Jamaica instead of emigrating to America. America destroys people, some believe. But every place can destroy people. Besides, maybe his suicide wasn't for him a destruction but rather a deliverance—or simultaneously both. No one knows, no one who is still alive can ever really know. He, the devout Christian, the [supposedly] loving father, the good boy who for so many years had taken such excellent care of his elderly ailing aunt [who, her infirmities and occasional hypochondria notwithstanding, ended up surviving him, though not for long]; the true family man who endeavored time and again to bring us all together, a sprawling diasporic family, across continents. His God finally didn't save him, but perhaps

such a stern God—the Old Testament vengeful God favored by fundamentalist Christians, who seemed never
to care a whit for compassion—wouldn't be able to save
anyone. I don't understand this, another cousin furiously
hissed, determined to regard the death as an act of murder
committed by the deceased's estranged wife—because
of course what else could it have been but murder, the
other cousin insisted in spite of the deceased having left
a note behind: *That's not something that we do*, the angry
bewildered cousin said, *Jamaicans don't commit suicide.* But
at least one of us did. Without any warning, completely
"out of the blue," as the cliché goes—or so it seemed and
still seems. With no indication of what might be coming
discerned even by his sister with whom he had always
been so close and with whom he had spoken on the
phone at least once per day, every day. When it comes
that close to you it's even more scary, isn't it? Because
then you think, well, if he did it—which means that it
is actually possible to do it, the reality of the act and its
consequences clearly looming as much more than only
the most secret fantasy of an uneasy mind—then so can
I. The act itself doesn't take much, obviously—just some
desperation, the right amount of sadness [or worse], and,
in the actual moment, decisiveness. And once you really go there, to the limit to the border, and then cross
over, then just like that—*snap*—it's done. You're done. It's
these latter thoughts, of course, that spook one the most.
A little scary secret, and very secret intention, for a quiet
solitary night.)

But all of that above remains in parentheses, at least in

writing, at least for today; as today, at least for now, feels (and this is a good thing) like something else entirely. Something else far removed from indifferent bridges and very bad feelings. Far from the secret planning of things generally best left unplanned. Nearer now to feeling instead that staying here would be much better. Staying, and, when possible, working hard on looking out. Looking out at this big wide world shared with so many others. Staying in it, looking out, and feeling very *here*. Joined. Feeling very alive, today. Until:

Without a Face

Not long ago, someone whom I have never met, but for whom as a writer and bold political presence I've long felt great respect—Mattilda Bernstein Sycamore—asked me to write a "short piece," I think the words were in the inviting e-mail, for an anthology that s/he was editing, centered on the various sorts of fears of and anxieties about homo men that one might feel, often does feel, as a homo man. Why are we so often untrusting and suspicious of and tense around each other, and what complexities might lie within these fears? (The anthology was eventually titled Why Are Faggots So Afraid of Faggots? Flaming Challenges to Masculinity, Objectification, and the Desire to Conform. And of course the startling question in the book's mordantly playful title is both extremely serious and powerfully radical, a question both daring and also one of urgent necessity.) This is what I wrote:

Consider this a kind of letter. A letter to you who, as one of those men, as all of them, I have watched and longed for and run from and wanted so much, yes: wanted and yearned so much, so often, to be like . . . to be like you: to be as lovely as you, as (from all appearances) admired as you and as popular, confident, calm, free, and (from all appearances) utterly unencumbered as you: light in your laughter, easy in your stride, and (often, though not always) so muscled. Muscled, lovely, young, and seemingly so indifferent to fear. You who (whomever you were from time to time) were often a kind of hero, a sort of god . . . someone and something to worship, as you remain, in fact, even after all the years . . . for in my very privatemost, most secret, and most very hidden realm, this is still how I think of you. How I think of you and all of them.

But then why? Why the fear that I feel at the same time whenever thinking of you, and why so much of it? So much, enough to bring a cold sweat (felt often at the most unexpected times); enough, this fear, to bring a trembling in the hands, an unsteadiness in the knees, and that heat to the face: that most awful heat, the heat of remembered shame. Shame occasioned again by . . . was it someone else's disgust this time? Your disgust? Your scorn, contempt, even sheer loathing this time? What was it? And why write about all of it? Why write about it when it still hurts so much to think about it—when it has hurt so much in the past to think about it and feel it and remember it? Remember it—

But please, I really don't want to remember it. Don't want to remember or write about all of that anymore. About him: about—as a place to start—that young man; that very young man, in fact just a boy, really, a teenager; in truth really just a child, naïve as he remained for the longest time—but never mind, then, all right; let him think that he was something of a man, almost one. Almost a man at fourteen years of age, or fifteen, or something like that; that child, standing there on some street corner somewhere, or walking quickly somewhere with, as usual, his head cast downward, though he loved the sky, loved birds, loved green things and bright colors and of course snow- flakes and even—in spite of everything—blinding white light. That child, brown boy, large-eyed, often clumsy (his legs and arms, rather long, often got in the way of his simply being); that creature at fourteen or fifteen or whatever age, always a bit scared . . . or no, in fact very scared. Very scared as, in those years, he began to seek out the places where they, those men who seemed to know so much and so much that was utterly unspeakable, and even, in his world quite different from most of theirs (he thought), unthinkable, congregated, passed time: big grown men who seemed at ease and not at ease with each other, and who sometimes embraced and kissed each other on the street—on the street!—in front of him, in front of others, not always caring . . . not caring, certainly, if they found themselves in places that they considered safe, on streets where they would not be killed. He had to travel far, so very far, from his own quite different world, in order to find them. In his each-and-each-day world of Ja- maican accents and North Bronx kitchens, that known world of grandparents who spoke regularly with the dead and people who it seemed could never forget that island from which both they and their deepest memories had come, such men were not—at least so he had felt at the time—very easy to find. As a child thinking himself almost a man (whatever that would ultimately mean; already he knew even as a child that it would be both a challenge and triumph to grow up to become a living breathing black man with body and mind intact), he found himself fright-

ened to look at them, those men—perhaps because, in those days, looking at them in the city so far from the North Bronx kitchens and island accents, so many of them were white, seemed only to be white; was it possible to be like them only if one were white, if one somehow became white?—as he also thought: Am I going to grow up to become that—to become them? But how do you do that? How do you do it? he wondered. I don't know how . . . how do you look into another person's face and let them know—let them know that you want—that you want to—

But then remember that this is a letter also partly about birds' wings. The birds' wings that he, that child, as he grew to be a man (an actual man and not the fanciful one of his youthful dreams), did not possess, and so fervently longed for whenever he found himself in the company of some of *them*: those men of whom, in his own very different way, he grew up to be a part, but not a part. (But a part.) The birds' wings he wished for to take him far and suddenly away from them—away from their eyes before which, in great shyness, he feared he would never be enough: *I'll never be enough for them, never truly wanted or really truly cared for by any of them*, he had so often thought. *They will always laugh out loud when they see me coming. I dared not look at so many of them, never into their actual eyes*, he'd thought, *because I so feared that I would find there the scorn and contempt that I had seen so many times before; seen when I was younger, when I was not younger. The scorn and contempt of Who is this little faggot, this little immigrant kid reject bitch looking at me.* (But in fact, according to the laws and the reality, his parents had been immigrants, not him. Did that mean that *they* had been rejects? Bitches?) *This little shithouse sissy faggot reject looking at me.* (Yes, because supreme masculinity, even with them, especially with them, had to be supreme.) *Who is this faggot looking at?*

Who?

But that was me. *(But it hurts. It really hurts, and why the hell did So-and-So ask me to write these words? And why, like a fool, did I say, Yes? Yes, I will write something about this, like a fool. But still.)* But since "me" does hurt, and since here also it is frightening and much too revealing to have "me" at last so exposed, let "me" once again now become "him," although without birds' wings.

Without birds' wings to fly away whenever, in years to come, he was around them: at parties, at gatherings, in public places. He was around so many of them who, lovely as they were, tall as they often were, broad as they so often were, made it clear to him time and time again—didn't they?—that they had absolutely no use for his limper-than-limp wrist, for his embarrassing st-st-st-st-stutter, for his "girly" faggy laugh. ("Damn, man, even when you laugh *you sound like a faggot. What the fuck?" one of them had once said to him . . . in the teen years, in the very difficult years.) Be a man, be a fucking man, so many of them had said, but how do you do that? he had always wanted to know. Can you show me, I just don't know. Nobody knows. He couldn't know then that they themselves were ashamed, and more ashamed, of all that they had learned to be ashamed of, beginning with their own wrists and the swing of their own hips, forcefully quietened by many of them in the pursuit of true,* true *manhood. But all that would be only the beginning of so many*

*things for him. And the end? But there would be (though he
could not know this at the time) no foreseeable ending.*

*"I suppose I was afraid" (he wrote; found in a bottle
tossed out to sea many years after his death; the bottle
and its contents now situated in the Museum of Utter Truths, in the northernmost region of yet another
global and ever-shifting region of dreams) "—afraid of
them because I wanted so many of them, you see—so
many—just to love me. Yes, just to love—that was all.
Just to look at me,* look *at me, and say, in words or
with their eyes, 'Well . . . well, okay. You, wonderful. Yes,
of course.' To look at me and say, in words or in other
ways, 'But this will be just fine. This one (large-ish
eyes, and a little awkward, but never mind, all right)
will be just enough.' I wanted to say those things too.
To hold out my arms and hold him—hold* them. *Perhaps I even wanted to sing then when I began to feel
that way about one of them; and I suppose in that way,
so given to joys of the heart in celebration as I have
always been, I have always been a bit of a fool—what
some call a dreamer, I know. But I speak what I know
was* felt, *and felt again. I never wanted to talk with
one of them and find, as had happened on more than
one occasion, that his eyes traveled in so many different
directions whenever another man came into the room, or
walked by. I never wanted him, or any of them, to feel
embarrassed about being near me because of my wrists,
or my voice, or my 'mannerisms,' as one of them termed
such things. I just . . . but, well. For most if not all of*

them despised anything that they considered not utterly masculine . . . anything else was hateful, loathsome. But then some of them, when it came to—"

[The remaining contents of this note are indecipherable, having been blurred and smudged by the sea over time. The sea, perhaps mercifully, has erased the writer's memory and even identity. Thus some sadness, and perhaps even a small register of grief, have been wiped out, obliterated, and pulled,

pulled,

down to the bottom of the sea.]

(Present Day; A Faceless Voice)

It's nice, really nice, when you can speak about troubling things without a face. In this way, you can say all the things that you might at some point have been afraid to say, without anyone knowing how you really feel. When you speak facelessly, you don't have to worry about the birds' wings you always wanted—needed—for your flight and safety, but never managed to secure. You can look at people without them really seeing you, and live, I mean really *live*, without them really seeing you—and if that isn't safety, what is?

These days, in the faceless time, I love watching them walk down the street holding hands. Holding each other. Kissing each other. Saying things to each other that only they can understand. I'm invisible to them now, more than ever, maybe, so what I'm feeling when I see them doesn't matter, because whatever I'm feeling won't show

on the face that I haven't got. Since I'm invisible, I don't
have to be afraid anymore. It's like now I know that none
of them, not even the handsomest or the most stylish one,
will look at me with that What-the-fuck-is-*he*-looking-at
expression. So now I really love watching them, wondering as I watch what it's like to feel all the things they
must feel together. All the things they probably feel as
they hold each other and are just together. As they touch
each other again and again, and say things like (listen to
them, listen!)—things like "_____"; things like that,
for instance, that you can't really describe or write down
because there's always so much, isn't there, in the not-said
thing, and in the breath between. So much in the look,
the look that both precedes and follows the very chosen
word. I think that you can read all about this in books,
though. Read about what all these things feel like and
what people who enjoy all these things call all of it: the
feelings, the being, the . . . I guess it's what you would call
joy. You can listen to people sing their voices raw about
all these things in so many songs, and go see plays and
movies that are all about it. After a while, thinking about
all these things, you begin to understand how important
the joy thing really is to people—to people who have
faces and even to some who don't.

If I were to tell the truth (which I might not try to
do even if I had a face), I'd say that I'd be really afraid
of doing all these things, feeling all these things, with
one of those men—with a man—because, one night—
one day—I might dare to look right at him, right into
his eyes, and see that he really did like me; that, in fact,

he more than liked me, as I'd been hoping so much he would and had been so fearful he would; as I had felt all those things for him. (Would that be what everyone calls joy? I just don't know.) Even if I had a face, a real one, I would never dare say that I can still hear all those voices from those earlier years, and see the scornful eyes, the disgusted mouths, and especially see how their mouths curl just before they say something like, "Faggot," or, "What a little bitch," even though they, the ones saying it, are "faggots" themselves, or will soon be. With my own face on, I would never admit that I can still hear and see and feel all that, the same way I know that it's all still deep-twisted up and twined in me, barbed and crooked . . . the same way I know that it still jabs sharply into me now and again, sharp, *little faggot*, whenever I turn the wrong way, this way or that, on the bed, on the big old there-it-is-and-always-will-be my bed.

And, well, you know . . . especially with my own face on, there's no way I would ever dare talk about how I want to put my hand out—put it out to many of them, yes, but especially to him. To him right there, standing right there the way he always does in the frontmost part of my dreams. Can you see him? He's there, sure enough . . . maybe not waiting for me, but at least . . . And if I could, maybe just one time, I would, looking at him in the dream the way I've always wanted to—I would just try to be—

What? Be *what*?

Oh, but I'm forgetting. Forgetting that I don't have to worry about any of this. That's the nice thing, one of the sweet things, about not having a face. You—I—can just disappear, or go way down into one of the deep places where there's never anything, where there's never anyone at all. At least not anyone who speaks.

Or just move on. Leaving everything behind.

Walking.

Not stopping.

Without a face.

Nowhere.

FROM ENGLAND: DISSENT, JOY, AND THE PAST THAT IS NEVER PAST

An Ugly Lesson in Repression at Cambridge University

In 2012, I was a Visiting Fellow at Cambridge University. On March 21, I participated in a silent protest attended by more than one hundred Cambridge students and several lecturers, in response to the university's recent rustication—temporary expelling—of one of its PhD students, Owen Holland. In November of 2011, Holland, with a number of other students and some lecturers, committed the grave crime of expressing quite vocal but peaceful dissent during a visit to the university by Conservative Party politician and minister of state for universities and science David Willetts.

The punishment that Cambridge decided to enforce against Holland for his protest, by way of its Court of Discipline and University Advocate, was draconian to say the least: suspension from the university for seven terms, or roughly two and a half years, a period of time that would deeply disable and derail Holland's career as it simultaneously isolated him from his Cambridge colleagues and the university's resources (such as reliable access to libraries, colloquia, symposia, lectures, etc.) that a doctoral student needs for the enhancement and completion of his research.

Many people in the United Kingdom—myself included, as an observing visitor—consider Minister Willetts's proposed cuts to higher education (principally what the Cambridge students and lecturers were protesting in November 2011) both reprehensible and deeply blinkered, and ultimately hugely harmful to intellectual and student life across the UK, from the more privileged realms of Oxbridge to universities with far scantier resources. For several years, in line with Conservative Party priorities, Willetts has aggressively pushed for government cuts to higher education and for universities' substantial raising of their tuition fees—proposals that, if ultimately successful, will result in innumerable students graduating with larger-than-ever loan debts, as the research and even teaching resources of university lecturers, and presumably the resources of other staff, are diminished. (Interestingly, in the face of these indefensible realities, in 2011 lecturers at both Cambridge and Oxford prepared motions of no confidence against Willetts, to be forwarded to the government after voting on the motions was completed. The motion passed overwhelmingly at Oxford, but was narrowly defeated at Cambridge. No-confidence votes against Willetts also succeeded in 2011 at the University of Bath and the University of Leeds, and in eight departments at King's College in London.)

While Willetts's problematic intentions are one matter of critical importance in the UK right now, the severe punishment of Owen Holland by Cambridge University—punishment clearly intended to make an example of him, targeting, discouraging, and stifling dissent—

is another entirely. What exactly did Holland—an articulate, thoughtful man whom I met during the 2012 Lent term after he attended a class to which I had been invited to speak as a guest—do to incur the university's strong-armed wrath? He recited a poem, of sorts, critical of Willetts's political intentions, and was joined in recitation by colleagues and lecturers, which action ultimately interrupted a public address that Willetts was invited to the university to deliver as part of—ironically—Cambridge's "Idea of the University" speaker's series.

As the event began, the dissenters in attendance were loud but peaceful, shouting Willetts down; the minister decided to cancel his talk shortly thereafter. While administrators' feathers may have been ruffled, no bones were broken, and the protesters brilliantly demonstrated not only the power and possibilities of conscientious dissent in a supposed democracy (one of the ideals of true democracy), but also opened a portal, whether the university was aware of it or not, to increased and necessary colloquy about the voice of students not only in the life of the university but in the nation and world at large.

And so for this action Cambridge University decided to pursue a course of extreme disciplinary action against Owen Holland (singled out from at least sixty protesters), the message of which was as ugly in its repressiveness as it was admonitory: if you dare to mess with Big Daddy or at least this particular elite Big Daddy, you had best prepare for retaliation.

Such repression visited upon another human being is clearly unconscionable, and especially so in an environment in which, ostensibly, humane ideas and discussions—and dissent—can, and should, be welcomed. The university's attempt to make an example of Owen Holland was deplorable in the context of one of the world's most venerable institutions that is still viewed as paramount for the quality of its education and its repeated success at developing and producing greatness. Indeed, greatness has loomed large in the numerous dissidents who have made their voices heard throughout Cambridge's eight-hundred-year history. Owen Holland and his colleagues, and those of us who recently silently protested his punishment, form part of what every healthy democracy requires: voices that challenge and critique what clearly is, in this case, abusive authority.

Ultimately, Holland's plight, and Cambridge's Goliathism against him, send deep chills to a creative writer who is also a political activist and intellectual: for if the university's ugly lesson here is that one should generally shut up and not risk disagreement, where does that leave those of us for whom the unfettered imagination's possibilities are our daily landscape, where there can and should be no proscriptive orders, and where, in the difficult pursuit of art, contention and disagreement will invariably exist? What does Holland's punishment signify for a Visiting Fellow invited here for a year to make art and engage in dialogue with others? Does it mean that, here at Cambridge, I should make certain to know my place and watch what I say? (Such possible harnessings carry particularly troubling implications for a writer who, like me, is black, gay, and a Jamaican American descendant of Britain's slave trade and colonizing past.)

In an e-mail sent recently to a friend, I remarked half-playfully, but also half-seriously, that I hoped my British visa for 2012 wouldn't suddenly be rescinded because of this article's publication. (Given the UK's present conservative political climate, the concern wasn't as farfetched as it might have initially sounded.) But then much better to confront injustice, I thought, and support the bravery of so many students and of Owen Holland in particular, than to bask without remark in a golden palace that, these days, discloses more clearly its insidious corners. It is an act of conscience and humanity for all of us to deplore and resist the sort of abusive power that Cambridge University attempted to enforce against someone who merely said, as was his human right: I respectfully disagree.

POSTSCRIPT: As of late June 2012, at least one part of this story moved toward a more tenable ending, when Cambridge University's court of appeals, the Septemviri, ruled that Holland's sentence would be reduced from seven terms to one. It is reasonable to assume that the Septemviri's final decision was influenced by the public protests and consistent, visible, and well-organized pressure brought against the original seven-term rustication ruling by the Reinstate Owen Holland Campaign—a group composed principally of Cambridge students, lecturers, other staff, and members of the University and College Union and the Cambridge University Graduate Union. Early on, members of the campaign alerted the

British press to Holland's situation and the university's original action against him. (Indeed, one wonders what Holland's fate would have been had the news of his severe treatment by the university not been widely publicized beyond Cambridge, particularly by way of the Internet and on-the-ground petitions.) It is also important to remember that, the more lenient ruling notwithstanding, the Septemviri, in its role as the university's appeals court, originally *supported* the harsher ruling handed down by the university's court of discipline. Waseem Yaqoob, a student quoted in the *Cambridge Student* newspaper in June 2012, observed after the Septemviri's final decision that "Owen's experience points to a worrying willingness in parts of the university to victimize and prioritize deterrence over and above other considerations of justice, and to a hardening of the university's attitude toward freedom of speech and action in protest." While Yaqoob's observation is absolutely correct, I applaud once again the efforts of all who, in the interest of justice, challenged the power of a formidable institution whose presiding officers, by way of official university channels, sought in this instance to make an example of one individual in an attempt to reinscribe Cambridge's ability and power to stifle criticism and discourage dissent.

Toward Joy and Writing: Snow in London, January 6, 2010
(Concerning mainly Finsbury Park)

———

Magical, for sure. And all a visitor wishes to do just now is attempt to capture it for a moment: capture the magic of that afternoon that has quickly become this one, as the snow falls down, continues falling: falling white, thick, now thicker, faster, blurring everything—blurring and veiling; blurring even the view across Finsbury Park of the red city buses on Seven Sisters Road; blurring all that and more here in this city where on so many previous trips a visitor has seen rain, only rain, although, to the surprise of many, sometimes much sun in the summer, and lovely warm days, filled with hours of birds fluttering; filled with hours of people laughing and calling and shouting in the park—as, well-dressed for the weather, here they are today, doing exactly that, doing all that and more with their children—but their cries and shouts seem somehow muffled in all this falling whiteness; muffled as are blurred the black wrought-iron spiked fences that surround the park. And magical, all this, to the visitor who loves this city and who only last week came to it for a month's visit (plus or minus a few days) after having spent the Christmas holidays in Jamaica where things are not so good by any means for so many people these days . . . Jamaica, where the colors were vibrant as always, beyond stunning, in fact, but where many people, including some dearly loved, were on edge often because of the crime, the perennial and unceasing crime . . . the crime that, unsurprisingly in Jamaica, murdered people and broke into their homes as they slept, as birds and butterflies fluttered over the island in the same way birds fluttered last summer when the visitor was here on one of his now regular four or five trips each year, as the birds—a small flock of dusky pigeons—fluttered in one great swoop from a rooftop on a building on Seven Sisters Road over to the park, and then into it, to somewhere well within it: swooped in seeking shelter, perhaps, or food. The visitor watched them and marveled, even reveled, in the small perfectness of their arc and design. *Beautiful*, he thought, *and so simple*. Just there. They swooped into the park not knowing then that umbrellas would not do any visitor much good on a snowy day like this one. The head *will* be whitened by snow in spite of an umbrella, the snow will seek out the head and frost it in spite of the best intentions . . . and how quiet the park was as various travelers on that summer afternoon of the arcing pigeons walked back through it toward Oxford Road North, heading back to Tollington Park Road (that street, like the busy Seven Sisters Road and Stroud Green Road on the other side of the park, appearing to be quite clear of snow today— too much traffic, perhaps, to really permit accumulation) and the quiet side street, just back of the park, where the traveler stays when here; and although, as the snow continues to fall and veil and whiten, the people in the park shouting and laughing with their children, and some of them not with children, and some of them with dogs and with children, seem a bit quieter at 14:45; at this hour all seems just a little more quiet, just a little more snowed-in. A little more hushed. Hushed, but for the occasional dog barking, barking and barking—that one, there, or that one, leaping to catch a snowball. Leaping in order to catch in its mouth the retreating afternoon.

Today is January 6, the Feast of the Epiphany, which I the visitor do not officially observe, although, raised as a Catholic, I well remember it. Well remember the scents of frankincense and myrrh, and the lovely small beckoning candles in church, in their red glass containers, in their containers of cobalt glass. But that is all mostly part of another history: mine, but in a different country entirely, though one connected historically to this one: the warmer one in which as a visitor I spent the Christmas holidays among the people, my people, who, as more of my many people whom I do not know, are present in this today-snowy city, bustling along Stroud Green Road; bustling along the roads and through the tubes, on their way from work, to work, to shopping, from market, to their children's schools, to home, from nearby home, to . . . One of them, a kind older man, bus driver, offered kindness the other evening when, as a visitor, I was lost in the Archway area; he provided a lift on his bus toward the next stop where, he said, a visitor could catch the bus back to Finsbury Park. I wanted especially to remember him: brown smiling face in a big red bus, his hands old and long and in their length and smoothness quite beautiful to look at. The hands of one of my grandfathers in another time, plunged daily into the yielding earth of that warmer place.

And they, the people of the warmer place, and others are still bustling through the whirling and quietening snow; bustling, but stepping more carefully now through the thickening snow. Stepping carefully on their way to or from work caring for other people's children or parents or grandparents, or cooking meals in other people's kitchens, in other people's homes, or, as the years have passed, increasingly in their own kitchens, in their own restaurants, their own offices and firms—their own places in a place that more often than not did not, in the most ugly ways, welcome them. The London Transport Museum's exhibits tell part of the story about how people of African descent, and especially Caribbean people, so many of them public transport workers in earlier decades and still today, helped to make this city what it is now; bustling along, their heads bent against the snow, Barbadians, Jamaicans, Ghanaians, Trinidadians, Nigerians, Pakistanis, Bangladeshis, Sri Lankans, Indians, and more, more, more, many more, for this is how the world should be, exactly: room for everyone, with a great deal of color. Color bustling through the falling white snow and through the gradual greening of spring's tenderness into summer; then through, and through again, the slow and inevitable reddening of summer into autumn and winter's deep grayness, its lowering brows . . . its yawn into long nights and bristling brief days. And so in regard to flesh, now and for all time, let there be an enormous amount of brown, a huge quantity of black, an unending amount of yellow and red, an infinite amount of all colors in between. Let the people in one million colors continue to bustle and colonize the Empire in reverse, as Miss Lou told us, as the snow continues to swirl and descend. As the afternoon dims.

Dims, shortens, wanes, as the trains from King's Cross hurtle through the snow beneath the underpass just at this side's entrance to Finsbury Park, bound for Cambridge, Peterborough, and many other places; they seem not to slow down in the snow; they continue, and indeed, you can hear them from the park; you can always hear them from here, snow or no snow. Now the afternoon, dimming, also sighs—for at 15:58, darkness is already encroaching. Today, mesmerized by the snow which in fact began in this city last night, as it began in the northern part of the country (someone who tried to drive down from the Cotswolds last night to visit had to turn back, the roads were so bad), one of the truly lovely things that is happening is that finally, at long last, the rapt visitor so snow-mesmerized is losing himself again, ceasing to exist as himself again, in the process of beginning to write again: to write about those people, whichever people, his people: all of these people imagined or actual (and, God help you, somewhere in the vast space of between); to write about the golden- or fluorescent-lit halal shops on Stroud Green Road or Blackstock Road or along Seven Sisters Road, the spiced desserts and meats hanging in their steamed windows; to describe how oddly "English" (whatever that means now, these days, in this time) some of the tube stations sound—stations like Highbury and Islington (on the Victoria line, the visitor's favored line, used more than any other except for the Piccadilly): "Highbury & Islington" sounding very much like that New York law firm in which one worked as a temp one summer: Cadwalader, Wickersham & Taft. And then think of some other station names that somehow sound so "English." Is it possible to imagine in the New York subway system such names as Walthamstow Central, Chalfont & Latimer, Dagenham Heathway, Totteridge & Whetstone, Pudding Mill Lane, Upminster, Tooting Bec, and Elephant & Castle? And then thinking of the tube again, remember how, although you told someone last night that you would travel down to Westminster or St. James's Park or Regent's Park or the Strand, or anywhere near the London Eye, to see how glorious— really beautiful—the snow would look on the Thames and its bridges, or falling over the ponds in those famous parks, or over other parts of central London, you didn't make the journey. You chose to stay inside and snuggle, to leave the rest of London behind. (And anyway, even if temporarily pretty, the snow would surely have been a mess on Oxford Street and along Piccadilly; it would have been an absolute mess in Leicester Square and the West End and Tottenham Court Road with so many people crowding the streets, as always. Central London, like many large northern cities except for those in Scandinavia and Russia and northern China, does not handle snow well . . . and anyway, glancing up at Westminster always brings back a bit too much of Empire memory . . . *But then remember*, an often-wise relative in Jamaica said, *that* we *helped to make it all possible: our backs, our hands, our sweat . . . Remember, and enjoy it all*, he said, *because we have already paid for it.*)

All of this—writing, seeing, remembering, picturing, taking "snapshots" whenever possible without an actual camera (the digital camera, unfortunately, left behind in the US), taking "snapshots" by way of writing—is a gift; a supreme gift that the world, life, the day (and then the night) give you. Part of the gift today is merely the simple ability, in these moments, to feel—to feel, just now, as dusk edges in closer, great joy, and delight in the world's often quiet beauty. In such a sequence of moments, the world blesses you. It says, unqualifiedly, *Do it, that's all, just do your work*—and in silence, no response necessary, a traveler can smile. Will smile. Smile partly because the work, this work, though often fiendishly difficult, difficult beyond description, in truth more often than not brings joy—joy while walking just now through snow-blurred Finsbury Park toward Seven Sisters Road, mouth hidden behind a favorite red plaid scarf. Joy gazing at snow-dusted tree branches; joy forgetting, if only for a brief while, the human, breathing, ever-dying self. At such a time as this one, mesmerized by whirling falling snow and by dusk's slow, very silky caress, a traveler just might close his eyes and whisper something like *Thank you*, then *Thank you* again, to all of it—to what has always breathed and moved hand-in-glove with darkness, and now slowly, inevitably, surrenders itself to it: the gorgeous, enduring, ultimately indescribable world. A traveler, finding himself all at once obscured in darkness for a length of time he cannot possibly know, even while rapidly folded within a cycle of descending snow that might never end and which he now tastes on his tongue, has, for certain, learned this much: that what remains of this afternoon—or of the days or years to come, or of any of it—cannot in any way ever quite be held. But in the place, just there, between absolute darkness and tightly closed eyelids, where both life and fear of annihilation begin, it just might be possible—at least so he hopes— that some of it, some small part of it, can finally, truly, hopefully be written.

The Bloodpeople Redux:
Just a Few Short Notes on Memory

━━━━━

Cambridge, October 2012

I don't like remembering so much of it either. All that viciousness and horror. All the suffering. The misery. The millions upon millions of deaths. The dead. But it seems morally repugnant to me, and also cowardly—and a deplorable insult to the disremembered dead—not to remember. Not to say, This happened, and we should never, ever forget it.

I will remember this year, 2012, as one spent in part among mostly very polite people. Among people who often, though not always, knew what the right thing was to say, and when exactly to say it. (Although sometimes they didn't, which ended up embarrassing one or the other of us, especially if the other person were white.) The people who often knew exactly what tone of voice to use in order to keep the conversation "polite," and which eyebrow, during which particular moment of irony or wry patter, to raise or maintain in its natural position. This was a year spent at a college at Cambridge, where one encountered many very lovely people, as well as some unfortunately deeply Eurocentric boors.

★ ★ ★

Lovely people, boors, and Anglophiles. A great many, it seemed, of the latter this past year. Anglo-philia: an adoration, idealization, of England, English "culture," "Englishness"? But what is "Englishness" in today's increasingly nonwhite, non-Christian England? Is this a question that the United Kingdom's British National Party and Aryan Strike Force, for example, wish rather desperately to answer?

But brickbats and homemade bombs are never good responses to questions asked in words.

However one literally defines "Englishness"—a state which, for the good of many, would perhaps best remain undefined, but also certainly expanded—the concept strikes one who wishes to remain aware of history as peculiar. For why do you love the English so much? one would like to ask. Ask, for a start, the American and Canadian tourists who fawn and gush and flutter their eyes at Buckingham Palace. "Oh, the queen!" some of them cry. "Will we actually get to see the queen?" Then ask the tourists from everywhere, since many other nationalities, including those from Europe and Britain itself, gather regularly at the palace to gush. To gush, fawn, and pay tribute to . . . to what? And, in 2012, to whom?

Why do you love the British so much? a continental European acquaintance asked an Anglophile American friend. Because of their accents—the upper-class accents, anyway, including the accent referred to by some as "cut

glass"—that many people consider so mellifluous? So "cultured"? Put this question to the Americans and the Canadians, for a start; then put it to all those, everywhere, who absolutely melt before a cut-glass British accent. Who lose themselves in adoration and even worship when in the presence of such an accent.

Ask the Americans and the Canadians, and then everyone else, if they agree with the widely held (and often subconscious) perception that an upper-class British accent signifies great—greater—greatest—intelligence.

Advertisement seen in a Long Island Rail Road train, summer 2012: "Even the loudmouth next to you would sound better with a British accent." (For BBC America.)

Why do you love the British so much? an old black Jamaican man wanted to ask someone. Displaying such iconoclasm and also simple common sense informed by a formidable knowledge of history, including the many abhorrent parts of British colonial history, he was extremely unusual for a Jamaican of his generation: a "British" Caribbean person. Why do you love them so much? he wanted to know. Because they developed Oxford and Cambridge, and "permitted" you to go there? Because of their illustrious kings and queens? Because of the present-day royal family, of which so many people both within and outside of Britain seem unable ever to get enough?

★ ★ ★

Anglo-philia: it seems not to work so well when one speaks about colonialism. It seems to sputter and grow a bit feeble, even chagrined, when one speaks about slavery, and certainly about British colonial officers' and British army soldiers' torture and dismemberment of black bodies, brown bodies, white Irish bodies. Millions of bodies across hundreds of years. When one speaks about the histories that we certainly should not, in our present-day twenty-first-century beleaguered and always violent world, forget. Anglo-philia: it seems not to work so well when one speaks honestly about—when one wants to discuss the horrors of—the British trans-Atlantic slave trade. When one wishes to speak about (for example) the British colonial torturings of the Mau Mau in Kenya, of Kikuyus, and the British government's subsequent decades-long cover-up of the atrocities, and the government's destruction of vital documents that bore witness to the atrocities because of possible "embarrassment" of "Her Majesty's government." Embarrassment over Kenyans burned, Kenyan bodies flayed. Kenyans castrated. Kenyans raped. Kenyans forced to eat excrement and drink piss . . . perhaps the excrement and piss of British colonial officers? But we cannot know everything, we shall perhaps never know everything, since so many of the records that documented the actual day-to-day tortures were destroyed. What we do know is that the British were there: viciously, evisceratingly *there*.

What the Brits at that time called a "civilizing mission" in Kenya was actually a "dirty" war, of course—or in fact more of a filthy one, notwithstanding the fact that all war is (to say the least) filthy. In the mid-twentieth century. The period during which the British colonial authorities in Kenya forced all those thousands and thousands of Kenyans—Kikuyus and others—into barbed-wire detention camps. Into what were essentially concentration camps.

Many people will tolerate hearing discussion of "concentration camps" in relation to Europe, but their eyes will glaze over and their chins will stiffen, as their arms will stiffly cross their chests, if the term "concentration camp" or "forced-labor camp" is ever used in reference to the African continent and European violence against Africans. Many people will acknowledge that torture, genocide, and generally unspeakable horror—horror that must be spoken and named and described and remembered, if we are to properly honor and do justice to the dead, and to ourselves in pursuit of a more human future—did occur in twentieth-century Europe. Of course. We know this. But British-perpetrated torture, genocide, and generally unspeakable horrors on the African continent? Many people refuse to believe it. Or at least refuse to talk about it. And certainly don't wish to remember it. Such refusal to believe, to discuss, to remember, ultimately suggests that Africans, unlike people in Europe, are not quite human beings. That African lives, black people's lives, are of less value than the lives of those who died in European concentration camps.

★ ★ ★

(In 2012, a relatively young man—a gay man from Venezuela, living in Paris—tells me a joke, thinking for some reason that I will laugh with him at the punch line. "What separates the humans in Europe from the animals?" he asks, grinning. Answer, delivered with a loud laugh: "The Mediterranean.")

We are fortunate today to have books like Caroline Elkins's *Imperial Reckoning: The Untold Story of Britain's Gulag in Kenya.* (And how excellent that Elkins actually does use the term "ethnic cleansing" at some point in her text, since this is exactly what the British did, attempted to do, in Kenya and elsewhere.) We are very fortunate to have an unsparing book like Adam Hochschild's *King Leopold's Ghost: A Story of Greed, Terror, and Heroism in Colonial Africa*, that recounts in excruciating detail the unthinkable evils visited upon Congolese bodies for decades by Belgium's King Leopold and his crew. Black hands cut off at the wrist, black arms chopped off at the elbow, black bodies burnt and burnt . . . and burnt. The stench of melting black flesh still befouls the air above today's Democratic Republic of the Congo. One would not like to imagine older people's dreams.

We are very fortunate to have a documentary like *Kenya: White Terror*, a BBC film that shows interviews with some of the survivors of the British Kenyan atrocities and some of those responsible for them. Fortunate—yes, very—to have a book like David Anderson's *Histories of the Hanged: The Dirty War in Kenya and the End of Empire.*

And what a brilliant title *Histories of the Hanged* is. For it could refer to lynchings in the United States; or to other British atrocities someplace else on the globe.

("But what exactly do you *want*?" a relative from Jamaica asked. "Why are you writing about all this history that was so long ago? What do you expect? Do you think the British are going to sell Buckingham Palace or the National Portrait Gallery and pay reparations to Kenyans, Nigerians, Indians, Pakistanis—whomever?"

If I could have calmly responded to that relative's question, in which I discerned both hostility and impatience—a relative who himself, though relatively young, firmly if tacitly believes that the British walk on water—I would have said, quietly: "I don't expect anything. Not anything at all. I just want people to remember that no matter how much they adore cut-glass British accents, many, *many* terrible things happened on the receiving ends of those accents. Things like bayoneted bodies, incinerated villages, and white British cocks forced into brown, black, and yellow women's and men's bodies. That's all I want," I would have told him. "Just for people to remember. Remember the Irish as well: the Easter Rebellion, or Bloody Sunday. Remember as much as possible, while drinking Earl Grey or English Breakfast, and selecting these or those Fortnum & Mason biscuits.")

The British colonial officers were not happy about the Mau Mau Uprising (1952–1960). The Mau Mau, and many other Kenyans, were not happy about the British being there. Not happy about those white colonial officers forcing their way into the country and—as the British had done in virtually every place they had stomped down their plunderers' boots—pillaging the country for all they could wrest from it, including the skins and blood of its people, to the point not only of murder but also of genocide.

Recent news articles have disclosed that some of the colonial-era files that detailed British violence in Kenya were uncovered in a secret Foreign Office archive, and may eventually be made public.

So much of this violence occurring during the Kenyan "Emergency" years, 1952–1960 (some would say up to 1961). But also before, and after.

Anglo-philia: it works not so well when we start talking about the British castrating and burning Kenyans. Raping them. It works not so well when we speak also about the Brits' castrating and burning Indians, and raping them also. And to be sure there are all the millions of others: a voluminous list of those who suffered and died, and were tortured, in places where the sun never set.

Remember Paulo Nzili, castrated by the British in the Embakasi forced-labor camp, Kenya. But also how many others?

★ ★ ★

Remember Jane Muthoni Mara, a Mau Mau who as a young girl was raped *several times* in Kenya by British colonial officers. Jane Muthoni Mara, and how many others?

Jane Muthoni Mara, Paulo Muoka Nzili, and Wambugu Wa Nyingi, who finally this year, after years of persistence, won their case in the UK high court, giving them permission to claim damages against the government for tortures suffered during the Mau Mau Uprising. The two men in their mideighties, Jane Muthoni Mara in her early seventies.

Perhaps I feel even more outraged about these histories than I would ordinarily feel because it seems extremely difficult to speak about the history—calmly, of course, without recriminations or mouth-foaming—here at Cambridge, at least among many of the people whom I have known here, some of whose company I have often for the most part greatly enjoyed. Yet it seems that some of them, when one asks calmly, quietly, if they have read the recent *Guardian* articles focused on new information about British colonial torture of Africans and Mau Mau in particular, become deeply uncomfortable. That's when you notice that, holding tightly to their teacups, they begin to blink blankly. To clear their throats which in fact hadn't, up to then, needed clearing.

Excellent: that a lecturer at Cambridge whom I met this year, Priyamvada Gopal, used the term "imperial amnesia" in an incisive article in the *Guardian* about the British colonial torture of Kenyans and the present government's reluctance to deal with the consequences. Some of her words:

> [British imperialism's] legacies are unfortunately not all about railways, parliamentary democracy and the English language. In the Kenyan case, the building of the railway itself had grim consequences including mass displacement and thousands of "coolie" deaths. The creation of an English-speaking elite in India . . . still disadvantages millions. Can reparations really be made for what took place under colonial rule across Asia, Africa and the Caribbean or, indeed, closer to home in Ireland? How do you compensate people for the ways in which their circumstances have been shaped by stolen lands, enslaved or massacred ancestors, expropriated resources, imposed languages, forced labour, artificial national boundaries, geographical displacement, avoidable famines, discriminatory taxation or institutionalised racial hierarchies?[1]

The Native American author Ward Churchill came up with excellent titles for some of his books. We can apply them to the British Empire and slave trade: *A Little Matter of Genocide.* That one will do brilliantly, and is accurate in regard to the historically genocidal Empire. We can borrow also his *Fantasies of the Master Race.* When we prepare to adore the people with the mellifluous, sometimes cut-glass, accents, let us make sure to remember *Fantasies of the Master Race.*

When it comes to the British—and to so many others—there are so many stories to remember . . . but also so many undisclosed and buried histories to uncover. But the work is exhausting, isn't it? For they often—though not always—covered their dirty work so well. I haven't even begun to write about the literally countless nameless, historically faceless people who died during the tortures and murders of Partition. It's overwhelming. The sun never set. But everywhere you look there's so much darkness. Darkness, and British bayonets, and British truncheons, and British flames.

If a friend of mine who loved films were still alive, I would tell him:

Hey, you. How are you? I miss you so much. I miss your smiling, laughing face. It's been so long now since you've left us all behind, and every day's loveliness never fails to remind me of you.

I know you'll understand this, what I need so much to say to someone like you, because the Cambridge people for the most part around whom I mainly have been finding myself this year just don't want to hear it; and because even some people whom I know are friends and whom I know do love me, as I dearly love them, really honestly don't want to hear it. But you, being dead, have no problem hearing it, because by now, not only have you heard everything, being dead, but you were always one who despised blurrings, for convenience's sake, of the past that in fact still isn't—and might never be—past. And well, dearest, it's just this: only that I want very much to remember—and want the facts to be remembered— that amid the lovely accents and the delightful Fortum & Mason biscuits made by appointment to Her Majesty the Queen, the British did terrible, truly evil things: Nazi-like things, in fact, which isn't surprising, since their colonial regimes and outlooks were so eminently Nazi-like. So, for a cinema buff like you, I just want to say that in spite of Helen Mirren's remarkable portrayal of a traumatized Queen Elizabeth II in the wake of Princess Diana's death, and a moving portrayal of an agonized King George V by Colin Firth in *The King's Speech* (and I used to be a stutterer, you know that), the British committed innumerable atrocities throughout their Empire: acts that we should correctly term human evil. Maybe it's especially important that those of us descended from people who toiled for the Empire as slaves and as colonial subjects remember, and never forget. Important never to forget the British-imposed Kenyan gulag, as some recorders have called it, and that the British, like the Nazis, destroyed a great deal of evidence of their atrocities, although not all. In this way, dearest—by remembering, I think—we can indeed say something necessary, something vital, like *Wait: these horrors* did *happen here, and a great many of us know about them and have no intention of forgetting them. For there is, there must always be, a profound human usefulness not only in speaking or even shouting the truths of surviving memory to enforced amnesia, but also in knowing through every hour of every single day we have remaining on this sphere exactly where among us the most enduring bloodpeople exist, and which faces in our midst not only may still be bleeding, but also may ultimately triumph above all blood, flesh, and even fire.*

At least, so we must hope.

Endnotes

=====

An Open Letter to the Prime Minister of Jamaica (June 2008)

1. This letter was sent on May 31, 2008, to both of Jamaica's major daily newspapers, the *Jamaica Gleaner* and the *Jamaica Observer*. Neither paper published the letter. Bruce Golding stepped down as prime minister in 2011, and was replaced by an interim PM, Andrew Holness. Portia Simpson Miller, head of the People's National Party (PNP) in recent years, won the general election in December 2011. Prior to her victory, Miller, in debate with interim PM Holness, stated that if her PNP government succeeded in the election, she would soon thereafter "review" the standing buggery law and seek a conscience vote from Jamaica's parliament on the issue. Up to the time of this essay's inclusion in this volume, Miller has continued to make generally positive public statements that have recommended the development of more open attitudes in Jamaica toward homosexuality.

2. The comment by Prime Minister Golding to which I refer here occurred in the following exchange with

BBC journalist Stephen Sackur (entire interview archived at http://www.bbc.co.uk):

Sackur: Do you want to live in a Jamaica in the future where homosexuals can be a part of your Cabinet, or any Cabinet?

Golding: I want to live in a Jamaica where persons are free to conduct their private relations . . . but I'm not talking about leading Jamaica in a direction where its own values are going to be assaulted by others.

Sackur: With respect . . . that was not an answer to my question . . . Let me put it to you one more time. Do you in the future want to live in a Jamaica where a gay man or a gay woman can be in the Cabinet?

Golding: Sure, they can be in the Cabinet. Not mine. Not mine. Not mine.

Sackur: Do you want to live in a Jamaica where they can be and they should be and it would be entirely natural for them to be so?

Golding: I do not know that that is necessarily the direction in which I want my country to go.

"BUT WHAT KIND OF NONSENSE IS THAT?"
CALLALOO AND DIASPORA"

1. See Charles Henry Rowell, "Introduction," in *Mak-*

ing Callaloo: *25 Years of Black Literature* (New York: St. Martin's Griffin, 2002), pp. xxviii–xxix.

2. I first taught Philoctète's masterful, elliptical, highly allegorical novel in the spring of 2007, in a new undergraduate course partly inspired by a Jamaican friend who has translated the work of the Guadeloupean/French writer Gisèle Pineau, and with whom several conversations in Jamaica opened up enormous possibilities to me: the inimitable Betty Wilson. But the course—titled "The French Caribbean: Nations in Translation"—also began long ago in my imaginative eye while sojourning across the French Caribbean fields *Callaloo* has offered: plains from those of Aimé Césaire and Maryse Condé to those of Patrick Chamoiseau and Simone Schwarz-Bart; from Joseph Zobel's and Gisèle Pineau's fields to those of Edouard Glissant and Lyonel Trouillot. And more. This course, exceedingly demanding for the students and for me, has without question emerged as one of the most rewarding, fascinating, complex courses I have ever taught—a journey embarked on with abiding gratitude to the towering presence of the Francophone nations' ever-evolving literary corpus, and to *Callaloo* for championing works that have not, both within and beyond their national or departmental borders, consistently received the large, appreciative audiences they have deserved.

3. I couldn't know when I first wrote this essay that

only a few years afterward, on the heels of many trips to England, that—partly in pursuit of answers to some of the questions posed in this writing and partly in an attempt to deepen several of them while simultaneously widening and deepening my own diasporic geography, knowledge, and responses to all sorts of knowledges—I would develop a course titled "Contemporary Black Britain: Writing and Film." I would first teach this course in the autumn of 2011. While structuring and conceptualizing the course throughout the spring and summer of 2011, I soon experienced both dismay and delight (neither of which entirely surprised me) at my ultimate, somewhat grudging acceptance of the reality that it simply wouldn't be possible to teach in one term all of the existing black British literature available; to be sure, I would have been foolish, naïve, very stupid (or all three) to think that doing so was possible. (On the other hand, I certainly would have liked to have read all of black British literature in one term, if only to have that joy of reading and richness just for myself, students or no students.) And then another important intellectual question arose: how to present to American students—an audience not, as far as I could tell, at all acquainted with topics and history of central relevance to black British studies—an appropriate sorting of texts that might provide a broad but deep "representation," so to speak, of contemporary black British writing? A difficult question to answer, that one.

4. I think especially here of Ariel Dorfman's marvelous essay collection *Other Septembers, Many Americas: Selected Provocations, 1980–2004*; and, of course, of Milanés's famous song "Buenos Días América."

TOWARD A QUEER PRAYER

1. From Buju Banton's 1992 dancehall hit song, "Boom Bye Bye."

THE BLOODPEOPLE IN THE LANGUAGE

1. My aunt, Phyllis Monica Melbourne (to whom my book *Words to Our Now* is dedicated), died on September 21, 2011, at the age of eighty-nine, some months after the early drafts of this essay were written. When I think of her in connection with the word "here," I feel a momentary joy—for she was here, and she did live to eighty-nine years old, and these words, for a little while at least, can take me back to the time before things began, vis-à-vis her illness, to get much *more* . . . to get very much *more*.

2. Toni Morrison, *Beloved* (New York: Alfred A. Knopf, Inc., 1987), p. 244.

3. With regard to this testamentary stipulation, the exact language of Stephen Sharp Glave's will, dated
February 25, 1873, and probated in Manchester Parish, Jamaica, reads as follows: "I also will and declare
that should any of my children marry to any Black
Person, all bequests in this Will shall be cancelled and
be null and void, as also if any should marry contrary
to the wishes of my Executor and Executrix."

AGAIN, A BOOK OF DREAMS
(REFLECTIONS ON OUR CARIBBEAN)

1. The reality of a "queer" Jamaican population about
which I as a younger person had known nothing—and
one largely centered in Kingston, though of course
also found in other places across the island—was
brought dramatically home to me during the period
in 1998 when I helped to form J-FLAG, in Kingston. It was during this time that I met and became
friends with Larry Chang, well-known in LGBT Jamaican circles as a long-standing activist, and also as
someone who had willingly, conscientiously taken
the risk to be very "out" in Jamaica, even before
Brian Williamson, another J-FLAG founding mem-
ber and friend. (Brian was murdered in Kingston in
2004. The motive for his murder has still not been
identified definitively as having to do with hatred of
his sexual orientation, but many people, myself included, would not rule out this possibility.) Up until

that 1998 meeting, I had heard of Larry but, as far as I could recall, had never actually laid eyes on him. During our time of attending meetings and working together with the other founding members to develop the organization, I and others learned of Larry's having founded the Jamaican Gay Freedom Movement (GFM) almost exactly twenty years earlier, in 1978, in Kingston. 1978, when I was a deeply self-conscious, confused, sputtering teenager, convinced that, at least in Jamaica, I was the "only" one—whatever the "one" was or would turn out to be. (Whatever It was going to be, one had the frightening impression that It was utterly unspeakable, since no one, at least in my sphere, ever spoke about It.) What would it have been like to have known, as a teenager, of GFM! The stories and anecdotes about GFM's genesis and success were thrilling, fascinating, and often, in typical Jamaican fashion, simultaneously startling and wildly funny. What a glorious revelation, I thought, after getting to know Larry and learning about all that the earlier organization had achieved, and how visible it had actually been in Jamaica, even to the extent of its members and supporters writing frequent pro-gay, politically astute—and philosophically challenging— letters to the (mostly) antigay local newspapers. GFM also regularly published a mimeographed newsletter, the *Jamaica Gaily News*. Learning about GFM—or, rather, about how I had missed its time—also made me sad, however, thinking of how close I had been to the organization's members in physical distance, and

so very needful of such community and knowledge,
yet completely unaware of them.

JAMAICAN, OCTOPUS

1. I should say immediately that, in reference to myself,
   I disavow and shelve the term "intellectual," principally because it isn't a term that I have ever chosen
   or used to describe myself; because I wouldn't be
   entirely sure what, given my literary interests and the
   work I have produced so far, this term would mean
   or "ought" to mean; and because the word "intellectual" is of no real use to me when I sit down to
   actually write, nor after I have written, nor when
   I'm revising and editing. Yet, when in the company
   of people whom I do consider "intellectuals" (as I
   define the term, individuals who pursue an exten-
   sive and rigorous life of the mind and a principled,
   humanistic engagement with moral and ethical considerations that impact upon the world at large), I
   remain fascinated by the enormous possibilities of
   the humanistically intellectual work done by some
   writers whose work I have long greatly admired.

2. The somersaults of these more-or-less men were
   equally astonishing in that they were executed in
   groups of three, each group displaying the unnerving perfection of trained seals—indeed, as if these
   more-or-less men were invincible circus high-wire

performers. How much more arresting became the spectacle when I observed that, in their respective groups, each man held tightly to the fully erect penis of the other—essentially, it seemed, the man immediately to his left—in preparation for the somersault, during the leaps, and immediately afterward. But then imagine a small boy's further astonishment, even incredulity, when, at the end of each set of somersaults (the men always executed sets of four consecutive somersaults, which did stir up the sea-bottom sand at times), they engaged in autotomy, just like a threatened octopus might; that is, upon the groups' completion of the final somersault in the set, each more-or-less man's penis detached, apparently painlessly and with no trauma or surprise, in the hand of the man next to him, who simply raised the detached (and still fully erect) penis to his mouth, where he kissed it, then squeezed it gently. He then placed it very carefully and with the gravest precision firmly between his buttocks, where he held the engorged flesh as tightly as one might choose to hold contraband when traversing fiercely patrolled borders. Thus all of these more-or-less men continued their cavortings, postsomersault, in a penis-less state, with only a dark round something-or-other marking the place where, only a few minutes ago, their actual penises had stretched, bent, or (but there had been very few of these) drooped in a state of brief repose.

3. The work to which I refer here, and from which I

briefly quote, is the story "Out There," in *The Torturer's Wife*.

Andrew Salkey's Escape to an Autumn Pavement: *An Introduction*

1. The novel was originally published in London by Hutchinson in 1960.

2. Interestingly, Walcott's poem was published one year before Kenya succeeded in gaining independence from the British; many British Caribbean peoples living at the time in the Caribbean or in Britain or North America, Walcott and Salkey included, were keenly aware of the Mau Mau resistance and other anticolonial struggles in Kenya and in other colonized African nations, and in their own discrete ways participated in the trans-Atlantic anticolonial "conversation"—the cacophonous chorus of increasingly critical and dissenting voices—that was building throughout the British Commonwealth and elsewhere.

The Four of Them

1. See "Out There," in *The Torturer's Wife*.

THE BLOODPEOPLE REDUX:
JUST A FEW SHORT NOTES ON MEMORY

1. Priyamvada Gopal, "Mau Mau Verdict: Britain Must Undo Its Imperial Amnesia," *Guardian,* July 31, 2012 (http://www.guardian.co.uk/commentisfree/2012/jul/31/mau-mau-britain-imperial-amnesia).

ACKNOWLEDGMENTS

Two of the works in this book originated as public addresses. Some others previously appeared in slightly different form in the publications listed below:

"This Jamaican Family: The Word, and Dreams": *African American Review*, Vol. 42, No. 2 (Summer 2008).

"An Open Letter to the Prime Minister of Jamaica (June 2008)": *Callaloo*, Vol. 31, No. 4 (Fall 2008).

"'But What Kind of Nonsense Is That?' *Callaloo* and Diaspora": *Callaloo*, Vol. 30, No. 2 (Spring 2007).

"Toward a Queer Prayer": originally delivered in slightly different form as an address at the Oslo Freedom Forum human rights conference, Oslo, Norway, May 10, 2011, under the title "Ending Anti-Gay Violence in Jamaica." Published in *Liberalen* magazine (Oslo), under the title "Jamaica: Toward a Queer Prayer," June 7, 2011. Reprinted under the same title in *SX Salon: A Small Axe Literary Platform*, Issue 6 (August 2011).

"The Bloodpeople in the Language": *Callaloo*, Vol. 35, No. 4 (Fall 2012). Reprinted in the *Kenyon Review* (online), Fall 2012.

"Jamaican, Octopus": originally written for and delivered in slightly different form as a plenary address for the "Love, Sex, Desire and the (Post)Colonial" conference, University of London, Institute of English Studies,

October 28, 2011. Published in *Callaloo*, Vol. 35, No. 2 (Spring 2012).

"Meditation (on 'Barebacking')": *Bloom*, Vol. 4, No. 1 (Spring 2012).

"Without a Face": *Why Are Faggots So Afraid of Faggots? Flaming Challenges to Masculinity, Objectification, and the Desire to Conform* (AK Press, 2012; ed. Mattilda Bernstein Sycamore).

"Andrew Salkey's *Escape to an Autumn Pavement*: An Introduction": *Escape to an Autumn Pavement* by Andrew Salkey (Peepal Tree Press, Caribbean Modern Classics Series, 2009).

"The Four of Them": *Who's Yer Daddy? Gay Writers Celebrate their Mentors and Forerunners* (University of Wisconsin Press, 2012; eds. Jim Elledge and David Groff).

"Interview with the Not-Poem": the *Kenyon Review*, Vol. XXV, No. 2 (2003).

"An Ugly Lesson in Repression at Cambridge University": the *Chronicle of Higher Education* (online), "World Wise" section, March 22, 2012. Reprinted in the *Huffington Post* (UK), "Universities and Education" section, March 28, 2012.